500 RECIPES FOR QUICK MEALS

by Marguerite Patten

HAMLYN

LONDON · NEW YORK · SYDNEY · TORONTO

Contents

Cover photograph by Paul Williams

Published by The Hamlyn Publishing Group Limited
London · New York · Sydney · Toronto
Astronaut House, Feltham, Middlesex, England

© Copyright The Hamlyn Publishing Group Limited 1962

First published 1962
Twenty-fifth impression 1984

ISBN 0 600 03401 1

Printed and bound in Great Britain by
R. J. Acford

Quantities in recipes:
Unless otherwise stated, recipes are for 4 portions.

Introduction

This book is intended for the many people today who like good food and yet at the same time find it extremely difficult to give enough time to recipes that need prolonged preparation or cooking.

Fortunately the modern convenience foods, frozen, canned, etc., are of such high quality that it is possible to serve excellent meals without spending too much time. It is, however, important to see that the family are well fed, for no diet is an adequate one which does not contain a proportion of proteins—meat, fish, cheese, eggs or poultry. It should also have plenty of vegetables and fruit and a certain amount of carbo-hydrates—bread, flour, etc.

You will notice that the cooking time is given at the top of each recipe. This should be taken as an approximate guide since it will always vary a little.

There are many ways in which one can save time. Chapter 1 will suggest a few to you.

Other ways in which one can save time are by investing in a pressure cooker, by using small rather than large containers—individual pudding basins, pie dishes, etc.

In preparing dishes where cooked vegetables are required, if you wish to use fresh vegetables, remember they cook much more quickly if grated rather than chopped. This applies particularly in the case of onions and carrots. Quite often time can be saved by doing one batch of cooking which can be turned into several meals. Examples of this are the savoury beef mixture (see page 55), and the basic cake mixtures 1 and 2 (see pages 78-9). The same sort of thing can be done with other kinds of food. When cooking apples, for example, a little extra fruit can always be turned into another pudding or a sauce to serve with meat.

There is, however, one important thing to keep in mind. No matter how busy the daily routine, it is essential to make sure that everyone in the family is kept properly supplied with the essential foods.

Some Useful Facts and Figures

Comparison of Weights and Measures

English weights and measures have been used throughout the book. 3 teaspoonfuls equal 1 tablespoon. The average English teacup is $\frac{1}{4}$ pint. The average English breakfast cup is $\frac{1}{2}$ pint. When cups are mentioned in recipes they refer to a B.S.I. measuring cup which holds $\frac{1}{2}$ pint or 10 fluid ounces. In case it is wished to translate quantities into American or metric counterparts the following give a comparison.

Liquid measure

The American pint is 16 fluid ounces, as opposed to the British Imperial pint and Canadian pint which are 20 fluid ounces. The American $\frac{1}{2}$-pint measuring cup is therefore equivalent to $\frac{2}{5}$ British pint. In Australia the British Imperial pint, 20 fluid ounces, is used.

Solid measure

British	American
1 lb. butter or other fat	2 cups
1 lb. flour	4 cups

1 lb. granulated or castor sugar	2 cups
1 lb. icing or confectioners' sugar	$3\frac{1}{2}$ cups
1 lb. brown sugar (firmly packed)	2 cups
12 oz. golden syrup or treacle	1 cup
14 oz. rice	2 cups
1 lb. dried fruit	3 cups
1 lb. minced meat (firmly packed)	2 cups
1 lb. lentils or split peas	2 cups
2 oz. soft breadcrumbs	1 cup
$\frac{1}{2}$ oz. flour	2 tablespoons
1 oz. flour	$\frac{1}{4}$ cup
1 oz. sugar	2 tablespoons
$\frac{1}{2}$ oz. butter	1 tablespoon
1 oz. golden syrup or treacle	1 tablespoon
1 oz. jam or jelly	1 tablespoon

All U.S. standard measuring cups and tablespoons

To help you understand metrication

You will see from the chart that 1 oz. is approximately 28 g but can be rounded off to the more convenient measuring unit of 25. Also the figures in the right hand column are not always increased by 25. This is to reduce the difference between the convenient number and the nearest equivalent. If in a recipe the ingredients to be converted are 1 oz. of margarine and 6 oz. of flour, these are the conversions: 25 g margarine and 175 g flour.

Note: When converting quantities over 16 oz. first add the appropriate figures in the centre column, not those given in the right hand column, THEN adjust to the nearest unit of 25 g. For example, to convert $1\frac{3}{4}$ lb. add 456 g to 340 g which equals 796 g. When rounded off to the convenient figure it becomes 800 g.

The conversion chart

Ounces	Approx. g and ml to nearest whole number	Approx. to nearest unit of 25
1	28	25
2	57	50
3	85	75
4	113	125
5	142	150
6	170	175
7	198	200
8	226	225
12	340	350
16	456	450

Approximate liquid conversions

$\frac{1}{4}$ pint–150 ml
$\frac{1}{2}$ pint–275 ml
$\frac{3}{4}$ pint–425 ml
1 pint–575 ml

*1,000 millilitres–1 litre
1 litre–$1\frac{3}{4}$ pints
$\frac{1}{2}$ litre–$\frac{3}{4}$ pint plus 4 tablespoons
1 dl (decilitre)–6 tablespoons

Note: If solid ingredients give scant weight using the 25 unit conversion, the amount of liquid allowed must also be scant. For example, although 575 ml is nearer to 1 pint (20 fluid oz.) when making a white pouring sauce use 550 ml of milk to 25 g each of butter and flour for a better consistency.

Oven Temperatures

The following chart gives conversions from degrees Fahrenheit to degrees Celsius (formerly known as Centigrade). This chart is accurate to within 3° Celsius, and can therefore be used for recipes which give oven temperatures in metric.

Note: This table is an approximate guide only. Different makes of cooker vary and if you are in any doubt about the setting it is as well to refer to the manufacturer's temperature chart.

Description	Electric Setting	Gas Mark
VERY COOL	225°F–110°C	$\frac{1}{4}$
	250°F–130°C	$\frac{1}{2}$
COOL	275°F–140°C	1
	300°F–150°C	2
MODERATE	325°F–170°C	3
	350°F–180°C	4
MODERATELY HOT	375°F–190°C	5
	400°F–200°C	6
HOT	425°F–220°C	7
	450°F–230°C	8
VERY HOT	475°F–240°C	9

Basic Methods of Cooking

Baking—Cooking in dry heat in the oven.
Boiling—Cooking by immersing the food in a pan of liquid, which must be kept boiling gently all the time.
Braising—Almost a combination of stewing and roasting. Meat is placed on a bed of vegetables with a little liquid surrounding, in a covered vessel, and cooked slowly in the oven.
Casserole—Cooking slowly in the oven in a covered casserole dish.
Frying—Cooking in a little hot fat in an open pan. Deep frying is cooking by immersion in a deep pan of smoking hot fat.
Grilling—Cooking quickly under a red-hot grill; used for small tender pieces of meat, fish, etc.
Poaching—Cooking gently in water which is just below boiling point; usually eggs or fish.
Pressure Cooking—Cooking at higher temperatures than usual, so that food is cooked much more quickly.
Roasting—Cooking with a little fat in a hot oven. Fat is poured from the baking tin over the meat or poultry from time to time, using a long-handled spoon; this is known as basting.
Simmering—The rate of cooking used for stews; just below boiling point, so that the liquid bubbles gently at the side of the pan.
Steaming—Cooking either in a steamer over a pan of boiling water, or in a basin standing in (but not covered by) boiling water.
Stewing—Cooking slowly until the food is tender. It is done in just enough liquid to cover the food, as the liquid is served with it and should be rich. Stews may be cooked in covered saucepans or casseroles, on a hot plate or in the oven, but always at a low temperature.

Chapter 1   Ideas to Help Save Time

Stocking your larder

Convenience foods: an incredible amount of time will be saved by either stocking plenty of the convenience foods, or buying these for quick and easy meals. Obviously one cannot store frozen foods even in an ordinary refrigerator without a deep freeze compartment. However, as these are becoming rather more common, a very excellent range of frozen foods will be found invaluable.

Shopping for dairy produce

Cheese   Remember that processed cheese keeps well, so you can always have some available. It is possible in some shops to buy already grated Cheddar and Parmesan cheese. However, drums of Parmesan can be stored for a very long time. Use only small quantities of this particular cheese because it is very strong. You should also occasionally buy canned continental cheeses for emergencies.

Cream   This may be purchased in bottles or cans. Make sure that you have bought the type that will whip if you need it for decoration.

Eggs   Keep a good supply available. It is quite a sensible plan when cooking eggs to hard-boil 1 or 2 extra, so you always have some on hand for quick meals or garnishes.

Milk Supplies of canned, evaporated or condensed milk are an excellent substitute for fresh milk and cream. Or you can get the bottled milk which has been sterilised to keep well. Some people use the powdered milk (sold for babies) in sweets if they have not time to shop for fresh milk.

Shopping for fish

There is an excellent selection of canned fish which can be stored for quick and easy meals.

Anchovies —filleted or rolled, can be added to eggs, or used for quick savouries to serve with drinks.

Herrings, Herring roes —for heating as supper snacks.

Pilchards —these can be used on toast, or for quick fish cakes. Mix with equal quantities of potato, coat and fry in the usual way.

Salmon —the cheaper pink salmon is again good in fish cakes. The better quality is good for salads, sandwiches, etc.

Sardines —in oil or tomato, these are a very rich protein food, and as such, excellent for children, who generally enjoy them very much.

Shell fish —these can all be used in similar ways to fresh fish. Use immediately after opening the can.

Tuna —this is often described as the chicken of the sea. It has a rather firm, dry flesh which makes it more enjoyable if heated in creamy sauces.

Frozen fish —practically every variety of fish can today be obtained frozen. Much of it can be cooked while still frozen for speed. Look out for the fish fingers or sticks as quick supper dishes. The herrings, kippers and smoked haddock which have already been filleted are also useful, because they can be cooked more quickly and eaten more easily.

Shopping for fruit

Fresh fruit in itself is one of the most time saving of foods, for it makes a perfect dessert with no effort at all. There are, however, endless varieties in canned fruits which will also save a great deal of time.

Apple purée —excellent for sauce or sweets where one is told to sieve the fruit.

Canned fruit salad —this makes the basis of a sweet if you add sliced fresh apples, bananas, oranges.

Frozen fruits —these can be almost as good as fresh. The secret is to use them when they are still very slightly frozen. They lose both colour and taste if defrosted too much.

Dried fruits —apricots, apples, figs, prunes, etc., are an excellent standby in the larder. A thorough soaking in cold water shortens the cooking time.

Shopping for meat

Canned meat has become of very much higher quality during the past years. It is wise to store the following:

Bacon —pre-packed bacon in polythene bags is a good standby, and keeps longer than the unpackaged variety.
However, once the pack is opened, the bacon must be used in the normal time.

Corned beef—can be served hot, or cold with salad (see pages 35, 36, 52, 63).

Ham —small cans of ham or chopped ham can be used in place of the fresh variety.

Steak —cans of stewed steak can be made the basis of many quick and easy meals (see pages 34–5).

Tongue —ox tongue or small cans of calves' tongue can be served hot or cold. Be careful with this meat when once the can is opened as it deteriorates very easily

Frozen meats and chickens —these should be de-frosted at room temperature before cooking. The ready chopped chicken saves time and can be used in a variety of ways. Look out for ready prepared steak or hamburgers (frozen meat cakes) that just need a few minutes' cooking.

Shopping for pasta

Canned Macaroni, Ravioli and Spaghetti —these are extremely popular, and with good reason, for they provide a quick meal and a sustaining one. The canning process tends to make the pasta very soft so do not overheat.

Frozen pasta foods —various ravioli and other types of pasta dishes can be purchased. Generally speaking they are better cooked in the frozen state.

Quick cooking macaroni —there are a number of quick cooking macaroni foods on the market. Do not think extra cooking improves them for they have been manufactured so that they need only a few minutes in boiling salted water. If you are accustomed to the old-fashioned variety which did take rather longer to prepare, you may feel you should automatically increase the cooking time. This, however, is unnecessary and unwise, since much flavour will be lost.

Shopping for spreads

Savoury spreads —the usual standbys include cheese mixtures, pâté, paste, potted meats and fish.

Sweet spreads —you will save a lot of time if you keep on hand a supply of chocolate spread as a quick filling in cakes, curd to go in tarts or sponges, and jams, jellies and syrup.

Shopping for sweets and puddings

If your family is fond of sweets and puddings there are many ways in which you can save time. Have a good supply of the following in stock:

Canned milk puddings —these are good hot or cold.

Jellies —the quick dissolving jellies take only a few moments to prepare.

Meringue and pastry cases —ready made cases can quickly be filled with cream or ice-cream.

Pudding mixes —the ones on sale today are of high quality. Also, they save you the bother of collecting the various ingredients and mixing them.

Miscellaneous (sweet)

Chestnut purée —as a sweet, served with ice-cream. It can be used as the basis for stuffing.

Chocolate or Cocoa —it can be used as a drink but also for quick chocolate sauce. Blend with a little golden syrup, butter and water.

Coffee —the instant coffee not only produces a quick drink but it can also be used as a flavouring. Dilute with a small amount of water or sieve with flour.

Cornflour —sauces, both sweet and savoury, which are made with cornflour, cook much more rapidly. Remember to use only ½ oz. cornflour for every oz. of flour.

Dried fruit —in order to save time, look for washed, already cleaned packs of fruit and chopped peel.

Nuts —it is possible to buy these already shelled and skinned. Make certain that they are kept in a dry place, since without their skins they are more easily affected by damp.

Miscellaneous (savoury)

Bouillon —or beef cubes or vegetable extract can all be used with water to take the place of stock.

Cereals —quick cooking rice saves a great deal of time. Ready cooked breakfast cereals served with milk are a meal in themselves.

Mayonnaise —not only useful for serving with salads but also the basis for a quick hot sauce to serve with fish. Heat gently in a double saucepan.

Sauces —**anchovy** (or anchovy essence) for flavouring fish sauces.

Sauces (cont.)	—**tomato** to serve by itself, or for flavouring stews. Wórcestershire adds bite to a number of savoury dishes.
Soups	—both the canned and dried soups of today are of first rate quality. The concentrated canned soups, used undiluted, provide a gravy or sauce for a meat or fish meal.
Vegetables	—although it is impossible to have on hand all the varieties of every canned, cooked vegetables here are some of the most useful. **Asparagus tips** for salads, hors-d'oeuvre and to put in omelettes. **Beans** both haricot, as a supper savoury, or green beans as a vegetable. **Carrots.** The whole, small ones are generally better in flavour. **Mixed vegetables** as a hot dish, used by themselves or added to soups. **Mushrooms.** The tiny ones are excellent to fry, grill or bake. **Onions.** The dried ones are excellent time-savers. They need a little soaking before frying or steady simmering in a stew or soup. **Tomatoes.** Small cans of tomatoes are very good for cooking, the Italian plum tomato having the best flavour. Concentrated tomato purée in tubes is one of the most reliable and quickest ways of adding flavour. Do not use too much.
Stuffings	—as well as buying dried herbs, you can also avail yourself of the complete stuffings now on the market. These just require moistening before using.
Potatoes	—canned new potatoes are available, and also potato powder. This is very good if re-constituted carefully, and directions as to the amount of liquid must be followed most strictly.

Tea-time specials

Making cakes is quite a leisurely business but you can produce really most appetising results with the cake and biscuit mixes on the market. In addition there are frozen sponges which just need defrosting and decorating.

There may be occasions when you have the oven on, and time available, in which case it is very wise to make such things as biscuits, meringues or a really rich fruit cake for all of these store very well and can be served without further decoration. All one needs to do is to put the meringues together with a little cream.

Cooking tips

1 Salad oil on a pastry brush is a quick, sure way to grease oven dishes, patty tins, etc.
2 Rubbing or cutting the fat into flour for cakes and puddings is a quicker method than creaming, and can give delicious light results (see cake mixture no. 1, page 78).
3 Pastry and biscuit doughs can be made ahead of time, wrapped in foil or jars and stored in the refrigerator, or a cool place, and used as required.
4 Green salads with hot meats, savoury puddings and pastries are often quicker than hot greens, and supply palatable crispness as well as the raw food required in your daily diet.
5 Covered roasting tins or foil on top of meat keep the oven clean.
6 A pressure cooker enables you to cook a variety of vegetables at one time or even to cook fish and vegetables at one time.
7 Use ice-cream as a sauce instead of a separate sweet. Allow this to half melt, then put in a little flavouring. Never try to de-freeze it.
Instead of making pastry, crumbled biscuit crumbs can be used to line a greased pie plate.

Saving time when working

1 Collecting utensils and ingredients on a tray before starting to make up the recipe saves footsteps and omissions.
2 Oven-to-table dishes cut down on the washing up and there are many to choose from.
3 As you prepare food, put saucepans, etc., to soak.
4 When you have finished the first course put forks, knives, etc., into jug filled with hot water. You will then find the washing up easy to finish.

Storing ready-made pastry or flans

Pastry can be mixed and stored either in air-tight jars, or in plastic bags in the refrigerator. Rub the fat into the flour and put the crumbs away. The next time you need pastry, simply add the required amount of water. You will find that pastry crumbs, if stored in a refrigerator, produce a lighter short crust. If you prefer, however, you can bake several short pastry flans and store them in air-tight tins, filling them as wished. The pastry – if kept away from cakes, biscuits or bread – keeps remarkably well.

If it has become a little soft, then replace the flan in the oven for a few minutes before serving.

Here are some time-saving fillings for these ready-baked flans:

Savoury fillings

1 Fry diced bacon, sliced mushrooms and sliced tomatoes until very soft, then top with grated cheese and brown under grill or in the oven.
2 Fry thinly sliced onions and tomatoes until very soft, season well and top with anchovy fillets.
3 Scramble eggs lightly, top with sardines and thinly sliced tomatoes.
4 Fry grated onion and grated apple in hot margarine, add 2 or 3 teaspoons curry powder, 1 teaspoon cornflour and 1 gill stock. Simmer for 10 minutes, then add a few sultanas, and diced cooked meat, sliced hard-boiled eggs, or prawns.
5 Heat 1 oz. butter and add ½ pint shelled prawns, 1 gill milk and 2 eggs. Heat gently, adding a pinch of paprika pepper, salt and nutmeg. When lightly set, pile into flan case.
6 Arrange chopped, cooked meat on a very lightly baked flan case. Beat an egg, add 1 gill milk and plenty of seasoning and pour over the meat. Bake for 25–35 minutes in a very moderate oven (350°F.—Gas Mark 3). Garnish with sliced tomatoes or parsley.

Sweet fillings

1 Fill the flan with lemon curd. Top with a thick layer of desiccated coconut and brown under a low grill.
2 Spread flan with redcurrant jelly. Mash 3 or 4 bananas, mix with a little whipped cream, sugar and lemon juice. Spread on the jelly, top with more redcurrant jelly.
3 Grate 3 dessert apples, add a good tablespoon sugar and 2 stiffly beaten egg whites. Put into a crisp cooked flan and top with cream or ice-cream.

Chapter 2

Soups and Hors-d'oeuvre

Soup is one of the most warming and satisfying first courses of a meal. Indeed, a really substantial soup served with crisp bread or rolls and butter and followed by cheese and fruit gives you a complete meal with the minimum of work.

Hors-d'oeuvre are also a very pleasant way of starting a dinner, particularly when entertaining. A simple hors-d'oeuvre gives a feeling of leisure to a meal and need not cause a lot of extra work.

Stock

Many recipes for soups (and other dishes) require stock. I have given the recipe for making stock in a pressure cooker. However, proper care of home-made stock is a necessary 'chore' even for the person with little time. *It must* stand in a cool place or be boiled daily.

Brown bone stock

Pressure cooking time   45 minutes

You will need:

2 lb. marrow bones	2 pints water
1 carrot	1 onion
1 turnip	1 teaspoon salt

1 Break the bones, put into cooker with all other ingredients.
2 Bring slowly to the boil and remove scum from the top.
3 Fix the lid and bring steadily to pressure.
4 Reduce heat and cook for 45 minutes.
5 Allow pressure to return to normal before removing lid.
6 When the stock is cold, lift off any fat from top.
7 Do not add potatoes or green vegetables to this stock otherwise it will not keep.
8 In hot weather store in a refrigerator or re-boil every other day.

Quickly made stock

The excellent meat or yeast extracts or beef and chicken bouillon cubes which are available give you good flavoured stocks within a minute. By combining small or larger quantities of the flavouring with water, you can give the strength desirable in a particular recipe. For example, if a recipe calls for 'white stock', use a chicken bouillon cube or a smaller quantity of yeast extract. In a stew where a stronger sauce is needed, be more generous with the beef extract or bouillon cubes.

Onion soup

Pressure cooking time   3 minutes

You will need:

1½ lb. onions	1 oz. margarine or butter
1 pint stock or water	2 oz. grated cheese
seasoning	slices of toast

1 Melt the butter in the cooker.
2 Cut the onion finely and fry in the hot fat until pale golden brown.
3 Add the liquid and seasoning.
4 Put on the lid, bring to pressure.
5 Lower heat and cook for 3 minutes.
6 Allow pressure to drop.
7 Arrange toast on soup plates.
8 Pour the soup over and sprinkle with grated cheese.
9 For leek soup substitute leeks.

Scotch broth

Pressure cooking time   12–25 minutes

You will need:

1 oz. pearl barley	salt and pepper
3 oz. onions or leeks, sliced	8 oz. diced carrot
8 oz. stewing beef	1 pint water
8 oz. diced swede	1 tablespoon chopped parsley
4 oz. sliced cabbage	

1 Blanch the barley by pouring on boiling water, leaving it a minute or two then straining it.
2 Cut the meat into neat pieces.
3 Put into the pressure cooker with the water and barley.
4 Put on the lid and bring steadily to pressure.
5 Lower heat and cook for 20 minutes.
6 Cool the pan under water and when pressure has dropped open the lid.
7 Open the cooker and add the diced vegetables, sliced cabbage and seasoning.
8 Replace the lid.
9 Bring up to pressure again, lower the heat and cook for a further 5 minutes.
10 Put the chopped parsley into a tureen, pour in the broth (after skimming off any superfluous fat).
11 If the meat is left in, this soup can be served as a substantial main dish. Or the meat can be served as a separate course.

Minestrone soup

Pressure cooking time   30 minutes

You will need:

3 oz. haricot beans	¾ pint water
1 dessertspoon chopped parsley	1 oz. dripping or oil
	seasoning
1 tablespoon grated onion	8 oz. tomatoes
	8 oz. chopped cabbage
piece chopped celery	2 oz. cooked macaroni
1 oz. grated cheese	

1 Soak the beans for 24 hours.
2 Put them into the pressure cooker with the water.
3 Put the lid on and bring steadily to pressure.
4 Lower the heat and cook for 25 minutes.
5 Allow pressure to drop.
6 Remove beans from cooker and retain ½ pint of the liquid.
7 Melt fat in the pan, fry the onion, celery and parsley for 5 minutes.
8 Add the chopped tomatoes, cabbage, beans, macaroni, seasoning and the ½ pint of water.
9 Put on the lid and bring to pressure again.
10 Cook for 3 minutes.
11 As soon as pressure has dropped take off lid.
12 Serve the soup sprinkled with the grated cheese. This is a very thick soup.

Fish chowder

Pressure cooking time   6 minutes

You will need:

1½ lb. fish – hake, cod or fresh haddock	pinch mixed herbs
	1 oz. flour
2 onions	¼ pint milk
3 carrots	seasoning
¼ pint water	1 oz. margarine

1 Melt the margarine in the cooker.
2 Cut the onions, carrots and fish into neat pieces.
3 Fry the vegetables in margarine for 5 minutes, taking care they do not brown.
4 Add the water, the fish (cut into neat pieces), the mixed herbs and seasoning.
5 Fix the lid and bring to pressure.
6 Lower the heat and cook for 6 minutes.
7 Cool the pan under cold water.
8 When pressure has dropped to zero open lid.

9 Blend the flour and milk together, add to the chowder, bring slowly to the boil, then cook for 3 minutes.
10 Garnish with chopped parsley and serve with toast.

Summer vegetable soup

Cooking time   25 minutes

You will need:

12 oz. mixed summer vegetables (include peas, carrots, broad beans, spring onions)	1–2 oz. margarine 1 pint water ¼ pint milk 1 level tablespoon flour

1 Heat the margarine in the pan.
2 Toss the vegetables in this, then add the water.
3 Cook until tender.
4 Blend the flour with the milk, add to vegetables.
5 Reheat until smooth, season.

Tomato and vegetable soup

Cooking time   15 minutes

You will need:

either 1 small packet mixed frozen vegetables (or can mixed vegetables or 1 grated potato, 2 grated carrots, 1 grated onion, few peas)	1 bottle or can tomato juice ¼ pint water (less if using liquid from canned or frozen vegetables) seasoning little grated cheese

1 Put all ingredients, except cheese, into pan.
2 Simmer until tender.
3 Serve in hot bowls topped with cheese.

Vegetable soup

Pressure cooking time   3 minutes

You will need:

12 oz. cooked diced vegetables ¼ oz. dripping	¼ pint water or stock seasoning

1 Melt the fat in the cooker.
2 Fry the vegetables in this for 5 minutes without browning.
3 Add the liquid and seasoning.
4 Put on lid, bring steadily to pressure, then lower the heat and cook for 3 minutes.
5 This is one of the few soups where it is better to cool the pan quickly by putting it under the cold tap for a few seconds. Serve either with pieces of vegetable left whole or sieve the soup and reheat.

Cream of watercress soup

Cooking time   10 minutes

You will need:

1 oz. butter 1 onion 1 carrot ½ tablespoon chopped chives or tops of spring onions	1 oz. flour 1 pint milk seasoning squeeze lemon juice 2–4 oz. chopped watercress

1 Heat milk with sliced onion and carrot and allow to stand for some time so that milk absorbs flavour of the vegetables.
2 Then strain milk.
3 Heat the fat, stir in the flour.
4 Cook for several minutes, then gradually add the milk.
5 Bring to boil, add seasoning, watercress, chives (plus a little yeast extract if wished).
6 Add lemon juice and serve.

COLD SOUPS

A cold soup can be a very refreshing start to a meal *but* it must be *really* cold, not just cool. This means it should be put in a refrigerator. Methods for preparing cold soup and the ideal quick soups to serve cold are as follows:

Jellied soups

A jellied soup should be lightly set, but never too firm.

Consommé. This is nice if jellied. A good canned consommé and most home-made consommé will set lightly when chilled, and will therefore need no gelatine. However, if the clear soup is very liquid, heat and dissolve 1 teaspoon powder gelatine in each ¼ pint liquid. Put into soup cups and serve very cold with wedges of lemon.

Asparagus, Cream of Chicken, Mushroom, Tomato. Make the soup up to normal consistency with milk. Season *very* well, and reheat. Dissolve 1½ level teaspoons powder gelatine in each pint of the soup. Serve in soup cups topped with seasoned cream and/or lemon.

Tomato juice can be jellied allowing 1 level teaspoon powder gelatine to each ¼ pint of the juice.

Chilled soups

Remember, these must be thoroughly chilled.
Tomato. If using canned soup, thin down with a little milk. Serve very cold, topped with watercress.

Chicken, Cream of Asparagus, Cream of Mushroom. When ready to serve top with a little well seasoned whipped cream.

Cream of Asparagus, Cream of Mushroom, Mulligatawny. Blend with a little cream and serve topped with tiny flowerets of raw cauliflower.

Cucumber. Thick cucumber purée is refreshing.

Iced soups

For iced tomato soup proceed as follows:
1 Add a little chopped mint and top of the milk to canned tomato soup.
2 Re-season as necessary.
3 Pour into freezing trays and when half-frozen, pile into chilled soup cups.
4 Decorate with sliced cucumber and mint.

USING PREPARED SOUPS

Ready prepared soups, both canned and packet types, are an enormous help to the busy housewife. These are produced from very fine ingredients and give an excellent flavour. If, however, more individual results are desired they make a good base to which you can add your own personal touches.

Bouillon Cubes. These are not only excellent for stock but also for consommé. Add a little sherry and individual garnishes.

Creamed soups – Asparagus, Celery, etc. These are improved by diluting them with a little cream or top of the milk. They can be used as a basis for creamed vegetable soups, by adding few extra fresh or frozen vegetables.

Green Pea Soup. This can be given extra flavour by simmering a little chopped mint and bacon in the soup.

Chicken Soups. These can be used in a variety of ways. Add diced cucumber and simmer until tender, or mixed diced vegetables to a chicken noodle soup and produce a quick minestrone.
Mushroom and Tomato Soup. These two soups. mixed together are very good.

Frozen vegetables. These also help to simplify soup making. Use frozen spinach purée for soups, and the ready prepared macedoine or mixed vegetables.

QUICK HORS-D'OEUVRE

Asparagus Canned. Hot or cold served with melted butter or mayonnaise and brown bread and butter.

Broccoli Frozen. Cooked and served with grated cheese and melted butter.

Egg Salad. Hard-boiled eggs, coated with mayonnaise and served with green salad.

Fruit and Fruit Juice. Canned or fresh. Served very cold. Grapefruit. Halved with sugar. Melon. Cut into portions with sugar and ginger.
Smoked Fish. Salmon. Served with lemon, paprika pepper and brown bread and butter.
Shell Fish. Prawns, shrimps, lobster placed on bed of lettuce topped with mayonnaise or tomato-flavoured mayonnaise (add few drops tomato ketchup to mayonnaise).

Mixed hors-d'oeuvre

There are many other ingredients that can be used to provide a delicious and easy to make hors-d'oeuvre. Try to have as good a variety of colour and flavour as possible.

Ideally this should consist of:
Something with a fish flavour: Sardines, anchovies, rollmop herrings, mussels, prawns, smoked salmon, fresh salmon, fish salads of any kind, cod's roe, cooked roes. Dress the fish with mayonnaise or oil and vinegar and garnish it with chopped parsley, etc.

Salads: Potato, Russian, tomato, sliced cucumber, corn on the cob, lettuce, watercress, celery, rice mixtures, etc. The salad should be mixed with mayonnaise or French dressing.

Meat: Diced salami, chopped sausages, small cubes or rolls of ham, tongue, chicken; these to be mixed with some dressing.

Eggs: Sliced hard-boiled, hard-boiled and stuffed, mixed with anchovies or the yolks mixed with anchovy essence, etc.
In addition use some of the ready prepared savoury ingredients which are such a good standby in the cupboard: pickled gherkins, cocktail onions, olives, pickled walnuts, etc.

Grapefruit baskets

No cooking
You will need:

2 large grapefruits	1 teacup fresh fruit in
sugar	season (except
mint leaves	strawberries)

1 Halve grapefruits, remove pulp.
2 Cut strips from top of skin for 'handles'.
3 Mix grapefruit pulp with fruit and sugar.
4 Pile back into cases.
5 Chill, decorate with mint leaves and 'handles'.

Grapefruit cocktails

No cooking

You will need:

2 fresh grapefruit or   fresh fruit in season
  small can grapefruit   (diced melon,
mint   strawberries, etc.)

1 Remove sections from grapefruit or open tin.
2 Mix with other fruit. Pile into glasses.
3 Sprinkle with sugar to taste.
4 Decorate with mint.

Grapefruit and orange cocktail

No cooking

1 Remove pulp from 2 small grapefruit and 2 oranges.
2 Mix together, add sugar to taste.
3 Put into cocktail glasses.
4 Decorate with cherries.

Iced tomato cocktail

No cooking

1 Mix $\frac{1}{2}-\frac{3}{4}$ pint tomato juice with 1 or 2 tablespoons sherry, squeeze lemon juice, seasoning.
2 Put into the refrigerator until very cold.
3 Put a spoonful crushed ice in each cocktail glass.
4 Pour in tomato juice.

Mock smoked salmon

No cooking

You will need:

2 large kippers   1 very thinly sliced onion
pepper   juice of 1 large lemon
2 tablespoons salad oil

1 Remove the flesh from the kippers in large pieces (quite easy with a sharp knife).
2 Put into shallow dish with onion.
3 Pour over lemon juice and salad oil, add pepper to taste.
4 Leave several hours.
5 Serve with brown bread and butter.

Melon cocktail

No cooking

1 Dice melon, put into glasses and sprinkle with sugar.
2 Or cover with ginger syrup and mix with stem ginger.

Pâté

This makes an economical but interesting pâté.
No cooking

You will need:

8 oz. skinned liver   pinch nutmeg
  sausage $\frac{1}{4}$ clove crushed garlic
2 oz. butter   (or a little freshly
pinch mixed herbs   chopped onion)

1 Cream all ingredients together.
2 Serve with freshly made toast.

Prawn and melon cocktails

No cooking

You will need:

4 oz. prawns $\frac{1}{8}-\frac{1}{4}$ pint cream salad
$\frac{1}{2}$ melon   dressing or
paprika pepper   mayonnaise
1 small lettuce

1 Dice the melon or cut into balls with a vegetable scoop.
2 Place the prawns in a basin.
3 Add the cut up melon and 2–3 tablespoons of cream dressing.
4 Mix well together.
5 Line 4 glass sundae dishes with small lettuce leaves and place spoonfuls of the prawn mixture in each glass.
6 Pour an extra teaspoon of dressing over each portion before serving and sprinkle with paprika pepper.

Devilled sausage

No cooking

You will need:

8 frankfurter sausages   1 teaspoon Worcestershire
4 tablespoons chutney   sauce
4 tablespoons   1 teaspoon lemon juice
  mayonnaise   lettuce

1 Cut sausages into thin slices.
2 Make dressing. Mixing chutney and mayonnaise, add Worcestershire sauce and lemon juice.
3 Toss sausages in dressing.
4 Serve on a bed of lettuce.

Fish is an ideal food to choose when you are in a hurry for it cooks very quickly; in fact it is spoiled by over-cooking.

As well as the fish dishes in this section smoked fish haddock, kippers, etc. lend themselves to quick and easy meals.

Frozen fish

There are many excellent varieties of frozen fish on the market. They are ideal when in a hurry, for they enable one to cook the fish immediately without filleting or cutting into pieces.

As well as the white fish, look out for frozen fish fingers or fish sticks, fish cakes and frozen shell fish.

Baked fish

Cooking time   as below

Most fish can be baked – but care should be taken with fillets of fish to keep them moist.
1 Butter the dish well, put in the seasoned fish.
2 Cover with buttered paper.
3 Add a little stock, milk or white wine to keep fish moist. Use this stock in sauces.
4 Bake fillets of plaice, sole, etc., for approximately 12–20 minutes.
   Bake cutlets of white fish for approximately 20 minutes. Bake whole fish for approximately 12 minutes per lb. (if stuffed, weigh with stuffing).
5 The heat of the oven should be moderate to moderately hot (375–400°F.—Gas Mark 4–5).
6 Put halved tomatoes, mushrooms, etc., into oven at same time, and cover with butter and buttered foil.

Cheese stuffed plaice

Cooking time   25–30 minutes

You will need:

	4 large or 8 small fillets plaice
stuffing	
2 oz. butter	1 tablespoon chopped
8 oz. grated Cheddar	parsley
cheese	salt and pepper
4 oz. fresh white	1 sliced tomatoes
breadcrumbs	
to garnish	
parsley sprigs	lemon slices

1 Wash and skin fillets of plaice.
2 Dry well.
3 Cream butter, beat in 6 oz. cheese, 2 oz. breadcrumbs, parsley and seasoning.
4 Spread thickly on fillets and roll from tail.
5 Place in well buttered, shallow, ovenproof dish with sliced tomatoes.
6 Mix remaining breadcrumbs and cheese and sprinkle over fish and tomatoes.
7 Bake in a moderate oven (375°F.—Gas Mark 4) for 25–30 minutes.
8 Garnish with parsley and lemon.

Chutneyed fish

Cooking time   30 minutes

You will need:

approximately 1 lb. fish (fresh haddock, cod or hake)	2 tablespoons chutney
	$\frac{1}{4}$ gill milk
few drops of vinegar	1 teaspoon grated onion
2 tablespoons crisp breadcrumbs	2 tablespoons grated cheese (not essential)
few slices cucumber or gherkin	1 egg
	seasoning
	1 oz. margarine

1 This is a particularly useful dish for, when cooked the fish is already in a thick sauce.
2 Put the uncooked fish into a greased dish.
3 Mix the egg, milk, chutney, cucumber, onion, vinegar and seasoning together.
4 Pour this mixture over the fish.
5 Sprinkle the top with breadcrumbs, cheese and small pieces of margarine.
6 Bake in the centre of a moderately hot oven (400°F.—Gas Mark 5) for 25–30 minutes, depending on the thickness of the fish.

Cod Portugaise

Cooking time   30 minutes

You will need:

4 cod cutlets	sprig of thyme
salt and pepper	12 oz. peeled tomatoes
nut of butter	1 tablespoon tarragon
1 chopped onion	vinegar
1 clove garlic if liked	1 tablespoon water
little chopped parsley	

1 Season cod cutlets with salt and pepper and lay them in a well-buttered shallow fireproof dish.

2 Add the chopped onion and the crushed garlic, roughly chopped parsley and sprig of thyme, covering all with the chopped, peeled tomatoes.

3 Moisten with tarragon vinegar and water, cook in a moderate oven (375°F.—Gas Mark 4) for 30 minutes.

4 Arrange the cutlets in a serving dish, reduce the cooking liquor by rapid boiling, taste for seasoning, add a few bits of butter and pour over the fish.

Crab salad

No cooking

1 medium-sized crab is enough for 2 people 1 large one for 4 people. Feel the crab when you buy it and if it feels surprisingly light for its size, ask the fishmonger to break it open – for 'lightness' often indicates that it is 'watery' and you are not getting good solid crab meat.

1 Either ask fishmonger to dress crab or open the main part of the shell by pulling up the rounded part.

2 Take out the skin-like 'bag' and the greyish-brown fingers, both of which should be discarded.

3 Remove all white meat and mix with the meat from the claws.

4 Remove the brown meat and keep this separately.

5 To make the salad arrange crab meat on bed of lettuce. Top with mayonnaise and garnish with tomatoes and cucumber.

Crab scallops

Cooking time   15 minutes
You will need:

1 dressed crab (large enough for 4 people)	4 tablespoons Worcester-shire sauce
4 tablespoons mayonnaise or salad dressing	½ teaspoon made mustard
little grated cheese if wished	about 2 tablespoons crumbs
	butter

1 Mix the crab meat, mayonnaise, sauce and mustard together.

2 Put into scallop shells which should be buttered first.

3 Scatter crumbs on top with a little butter and grated cheese and heat until crisp in the oven.

4 Serve with crisp toast and salad.

Cod's roe and bacon

Cooking time   6–10 minutes

In order to save time buy the ready cooked cod's roe.

1 Cut roe into slices.

2 Fry rashers of bacon until just crisp. Lift on to hot dish.

3 Add a little extra fat if necessary, fry the cod's roe until golden and hot.

4 Serve with watercress or fried tomatoes.

Cod's roe pie

Cooking time   25–30 minutes
You will need:

12 oz. cooked cod's roe	½ pint white sauce or anchovy sauce (see page 21)
2 tablespoons grated cheese	
1 lb. cooked potatoes	

1 Cut roe into slices, arrange in a pie dish and pour the sauce evenly over the top.

2 Mash the potatoes thoroughly, pile or pipe on top of the dish.

3 Sprinkle grated cheese on top and bake in hot oven (450°F.—Gas Mark 7) for 20 minutes.

Shrimp salad

No cooking
You will need:

6–8 oz. fresh or frozen prawns or shrimps	lettuce tomatoes
mayonnaise	

1 If using frozen prawns or shimps allow these to de-frost very gradually.

2 Toss the shell fish in mayonnaise. Serve on a bed of lettuce garnished with tomatoes, etc.

Creamed shrimp curry

Cooking time   20 minutes
You will need:

small jar shrimps	1 can concentrated mushroom soup
4 hard-boiled eggs	1 level teaspoon curry powder
3 oz. rice	
1 oz. butter	
2 tablespoons cream	

1 Boil rice in salted water.

2 Heat butter.

3 Fry onion gently.

4 Stir in curry powder then add soup and heat.

5 Stir in shrimps, cream and chopped and halved hard-boiled eggs.

6 Season sauce if necessary.

7 Serve curry mixture with the boiled rice on either side.

Crunchy-top fish casserole

Cooking time   15 minutes

You will need:

1½ oz. butter or margarine	½ pint milk
1 tablespoon tomato ketchup	8 oz. cooked, flaked, smoked haddock or other fish (canned if wished)
seasoning to taste	
½ oz. flour	

topping

6 medium slices (approximately 3–4 oz.) bread	2 oz. butter or margarine
	1½ oz. grated Cheddar cheese

1 Melt 1½ oz. butter or margarine in a pan.
2 Stir in flour and cook slowly, without browning, for 2 minutes.
3 Remove from heat, gradually add milk, then reheat, stirring, till sauce comes to the boil and thickens.
4 Simmer 3 minutes, then add fish and ketchup.
5 Season to taste.
6 Turn into a greased heatproof dish.
7 Meanwhile, make topping by melting 2 oz. butter in pan.
8 Cut bread into cubes and fry in butter.
9 Top fish mixture with fried bread cubes, and sprinkle with grated cheese.
10 Brown under the quick grill.
11 Serve with a green salad or French beans or peas and grilled tomatoes or hot baby beetroot for colour.

HOT LOBSTER DISHES

Hot lobster dishes make a delicious party or special occasion dish and the following are quick and easy adaptations of classic lobster recipes. Be extra fussy that your lobster is very fresh and do not over-cook, otherwise it can become tough. Use the small claws of the lobster to provide an attractive garnish and serve with plenty of lemon.

Lobster Américaine

Cooking time   20–25 minutes

You will need:

1 large or 2 medium lobsters	2–3 large tomatoes
	1 onion or 2 shallots
2 oz. butter	1 gill white wine
salt and pepper	1 gill brandy

1 Dice the onion finely and fry in the butter.
2 Add the skinned tomatoes, wine and brandy and simmer for about 10 minutes.

3 Remove all lobster meat from shell and claws, slice and add to the tomato mixture. Heat for about 5 minutes.
4 Serve with crisp toast.

Curried lobster

Cooking time   45 minutes

You will need:

1 really large lobster or 2 medium sized lobsters	1 teaspoon sugar
	2 oz. margarine or oil
2 large onions	rice and chutney
1 teaspoon mixed spice	6–8 oz. chopped cucumber
½ teaspoon cinnamon	1–2 oz. grated or desiccated coconut
1 teaspoon curry powder	½ teaspoon powdered ginger
½ pint fish stock	
1 tablespoon lemon juice	1 chopped clove garlic
	1–2 oz. dried fruit
1 dessertspoon turmeric powder	1 dessertspoon flour
	2 bay leaves

1 To make the fish stock put the very small lobster claws, the head of the lobster and ¾ pint water into a saucepan with bay leaves and a little seasoning.
2 Simmer gently for 20 minutes, strain and make liquid up to ½ pint if necessary.
3 Heat the margarine in a saucepan, then fry the sliced onion and garlic until just soft.
4 Add the flour, spices, sugar and stock and cook very gently for 5 minutes, stirring all the time.
5 Add the flaked lobster meat, the cucumber, coconut and dried fruit and bring to the boil, stirring well to keep a smooth sauce.
6 Lower the heat and cook very gently for just about 5 minutes.
7 Serve with rice and chutney.

Lobster Cardinal

Cooking time   15–20 minutes

You will need:

1 large and 2 medium hen lobsters*	1 tablespoon sherry
	½ pint white sauce
2 tablespoons cream	(see page 21)

* The hen lobster has a bright red roe or coral. The fishmonger will pick this out for you or you can tell a hen lobster by the fact that it has a very wide tail.

1 Remove the meat from the lobster. Dice this.
2 Mash the coral rather well.
3 Make the white sauce.
4 Add the coral and stir in well.
5 Add the lobster meat, cream and sherry. Heat gently.
6 Pile into 4 hot dishes or serve on a bed of rice.

Lobster salad

No cooking

Allow 1 small or $\frac{1}{2}$ medium lobster per person.

1 Either ask the fishmonger to prepare lobster or split the lobster, remove the intestinal vein, and the lady fingers. These are found where the small claws join the body and shouldn't be eaten.
2 Crack the large claws very carefully and remove the lobster meat.
3 One way of serving lobster for lobster mayonnaise or salad, is to leave the meat in the shells and serve a half shell on each plate, piled with lobster flesh and garnished with salad, mayonnaise, meat from the large claws and the small claws.
4 The second way of serving the salad is to remove all the meat from the body, dice this, mix with mayonnaise and arrange on a bed of salad.

Lobster mornay

Cooking time   15–20 minutes

You will need:

1 large or 2 medium lobsters	$\frac{1}{2}$ pint cheese sauce (see page 21)
1 tablespoon cream	

1 Make the sauce.
2 Add the diced lobster meat and cream and heat gently.
3 Serve on a bed of rice or with crisp toast.

Devilled crab

Cooking time   5 minutes

You will need:

dressed crab for 4 people	3 oz. breadcrumbs
1 teaspoon made mustard	2 teaspoons Worcester sauce
seasoning	little top of milk
	butter

1 Mix crab with about 2 oz. breadcrumbs, Worcester sauce, seasoning, mustard and enough top of milk to moisten.
2 Put either into 4 individual dishes or into 1 large dish or crab shell, top with remaining crumbs and butter and brown under grill.
3 Serve with new potatoes and peas.

Fish rarebit

Cooking time   12 minutes

You will need:

4 slices of toast	4 oz. flaked smoked haddock or canned crab meat or left over white fish or shelled prawns
seasoning	
4–6 oz. grated cheese	
4 tomatoes	
lemon	
watercress	dash of Worcester sauce

for the sauce

$\frac{1}{2}$ oz. flour	1 oz. margarine or butter
$\frac{1}{2}$ gill milk	

1 Make the sauce which will be very thick and will, therefore, need stirring a lot.
2 Add Worcester sauce and cheese, heat for 1 minute, add fish.
3 Meanwhile cook whole tomatoes in grill pan.
4 Toast bread under the grill, butter if wished, cover with fish mixture and return to the grill, browning this on the grid while tomatoes complete cooking.
5 Serve each rarebit with a tomato on top.
6 Garnish with watercress and lemon.

Fish cream

Cooking time   45 minutes

You will need:

8 oz. flaked cooked fish (cod, hake, fresh or dried haddock are particularly good)	cream from the top of the milk or evaporated milk
$\frac{1}{4}$ pint thick white sauce (see page 21)	1 egg
2 level tablespoons	few drops anchovy essence
	few drops vinegar
	seasoning

1 Mix all the ingredients together.
2 Put into a greased basin.
3 Cover thoroughly, tie down and steam for 45 minutes.
4 Turn out and serve hot or cold with peas and grilled tomatoes.
5 Garnish with lemon.

Creamed fish creole

Cooking time   10 minutes

You will need for 2–3 servings

$\frac{1}{2}$ pint white sauce (see page 21 (or can of cream of celery soup)	4 tablespoons cooked peas
1 tablespoon lemon juice or dry sherry	3 slices bread, toasted or fried
3 tablespoons sweet pepper strips (or chopped canned pimento)	3 tablespoons single or cultured cream (or extra sauce)
	$\frac{1}{4}$ teaspoon celery salt
	good sprinkling white pepper
	8 oz. flaked cooked fish

1 Heat gently together sauce, cream, lemon juice, seasoning, sweet pepper strips, peas and fish.

2 Turn into hot serving dish; garnish with triangles of toasted or fried bread.

Fish potato puffs

Cooking time	45 minutes

You will need:

12 oz. flaked cooked white fish seasoning	8 oz. well mashed potato
2 teaspoons finely chopped onion	squeeze of lemon juice
3 eggs	chopped celery (use a little extra onion if you have no celery
hard-boiled egg sauce	1 oz. butter

1 Toss onion and celery in the butter, mix with potato, fish, lemon, parsley and egg yolks.
2 Season well.
3 Fold in stiffly beaten egg whites.
4 Put into soufflé dish and bake for 40 minutes in moderately hot oven (400°F.—Gas Mark 5).
5 Serve with hard-boiled egg sauce made by mixing 2 hard-boiled eggs with $\frac{1}{4}$ pint white sauce (see page 21).

Fried fish

Cooking time	4–8 minutes

This is one of the most popular ways of serving any fish. It is important to remember the following:–
1 Dry the fish well and coat very thinly with seasoned flour.
2 Dip in fritter batter (see next column) or in beaten egg and crumbs. Shake off surplus crumbs or allow excess batter to drain away.
3 For shallow frying make sure the fat (which can be oil, cooking fat, butter) is hot. Put in the fish, cook steadily until brown, turn and cook on the other side. If using deep fat make sure this is not too hot otherwise the outside browns before the fish is cooked.
4 For shallow frying allow 2–3 minutes on either side, for filleted fish. 4–5 minutes for thicker fish cutlets or whole fish.
5 For deep frying allow 3–4 minutes total cooking time for fillets—7–8 minutes for whole fish or cutlets.
6 Always drain fried fish. Use kitchen paper. The latest absorbent kitchen rolls are excellent, but never use greaseproof paper.
7 Do not overcook the fish.

The ideal accompaniment is beautifully fried chips.

Fish to fry whole. Most fish can be fried whole but it is correct to fry small codling, fresh haddock, sole, plaice, trout, herring or mackerel whole rather than fillet them.

To coat in egg and crumbs
1 Add little water or milk to egg to make it easier to brush over fish.
2 Put crumbs into paper bag or on sheet of paper and turn fish in this, pressing crumbs firmly on to fish.
3 Use either very fine soft white crumbs or dried breadcrumbs.

Fritter batter

You will need:

4 oz. flour	$1\frac{1}{2}$–2 gills milk and water
1 egg	seasoning

1 Sieve flour and seasoning. Add egg.
2 Gradually beat in liquid.
3 For fillets use large quantity of liquid. For more solid cod, etc., you can use $1\frac{1}{4}$ gills only.

Fried fish in cheese

Cooking time	6–10 minutes

1 An excellent way to vary fish and to add extra food value if the fish are small in size is to coat in egg and a mixture of breadcrumbs and grated cheese.
2 Fry in shallow fat until crisp and golden brown.

Fried fish meunière

Cooking time	6–10 minutes

1 Do not coat the fish with egg and crumbs or with batter but instead with a very light coating of seasoned flour.
2 Cook in butter until just tender.
3 Lift out of the butter and put on to a hot dish. Add the squeeze of lemon juice or few drops of vinegar to the butter, a few capers and a little chopped parsley and cook gently until the butter is a dark brown.
4 Pour over the fish.
5 The most suitable fish are fillets of plaice, sole, portions of skate or large prawns.

Grilled fish

Cooking time	4–10 minutes

Most fish is suitable for grilling. Fillets of fish, unless very thick, can be grilled without turning. Whole fish should be turned so that it is cooked on both sides.
1 Make sure that the grill is hot before you begin cooking and keep the fish well brushed with melted butter so that it doesn't dry.

2 Never over-cook grilled fish.

3 For grilling the fillets of fish allow approximately 4 minutes, turning the heat down after the first 2–3 minutes if desired.

4 For thicker fish grill quickly for 2–3 minutes on either side then reduce heat for a further 3–4 minutes.

5 An ideal accompaniment for any grilled fish are grilled mushrooms and tomatoes which can be cooked at the same time.

Devilled grilled fish

Cooking time   4–10 minutes

1 Spread the fish with butter, to which you have added a little curry powder and a few drops of Worcester sauce.

Tomato grilled fish

Cooking time   4–10 minutes

1 Add 2 or 3 teaspoons of concentrated tomato purée to a knob of butter.

2 Spread over the fish and grill as before.

Maître d'hôtel sauce

No cooking

To serve with grilled fish.

1 As white sauce (see page 21) but use ½ fish stock.

2 Add 2 teaspoons chopped parsley and 3 tablespoons thick cream just before serving.

Maître d'hôtel butter or Parsley butter

1 Add chopped parsley, seasoning and squeeze lemon juice and work into butter.

2 Chill and cut into neat pieces.

Hasty salmon pie

Cooking time   10–15 minutes

You will need:

a good-sized can of pink or red salmon	pepper
small can evaporated milk	1 oz. butter
pinch celery salt	1 onion
	1 can peas (or peas and carrots or frozen peas)

for biscuit crust

4 oz. flour (with plain flour add 1 teaspoon baking powder)	1 oz. margarine
	salt
	milk

1 First make biscuit crust. Sieve flour and salt, rub in margarine, add enough milk to bind.

2 Roll out, cut into small rounds.

3 Bake for 8–10 minutes on greased baking tray in hot oven (450°F.—Gas Mark 7).

4 Meanwhile, fry sliced onion in the butter, add the salmon, evaporated milk, well-drained peas and seasoning.

5 Heat thoroughly. Put mixture into dish and top with crisp biscuit rounds.

Jiffy grilled plaice

Cooking time   5–8 minutes

You will need:

2 oz. margarine or butter	1 large size (14 oz.) carton frozen plaice fillets—
juice of ½ lemon	partially thawed, or 8
chopped parsley	small fillets plaice
seasonings	

1 Melt the margarine in the grill pan.

2 Season the fish and lay it flesh-side down in the pan.

3 Cook for 1 minute.

4 Turn with flesh-side up and grill steadily until golden brown and cooked, about 5–8 minutes, depending on thickness.

5 Arrange on a hot serving dish, add lemon juice to the remaining fat in pan, reheat.

6 Pour over the fish.

7 Sprinkle liberally with chopped parsley.

Kedgeree of salmon

Cooking time   30 minutes

You will need:

8 oz. flaked cooked salmon or canned salmon	3 oz. rice
	2 hard-boiled eggs
2–3 tablespoons cream or top of milk	2 oz. butter or margarine
	seasoning
toast	parsley to garnish

1 Cook rice in boiling salted water, drain and shake dry.

2 Heat the butter in a pan, stir in the rice, cream, fish and the chopped hard-boiled egg white.

3 Heat gently.

4 Season well.

5 Pile on to a hot dish and garnish with triangles of toast, chopped egg yolk and parsley.

Oven 'fried' fish

Cooking time   15–25 minutes

Although it takes a little longer to cook fish this way in the oven it needs no attention and also far less fat is required.

1 Coat the fish in egg and breadcrumbs, not in batter.

2 Grease the baking tin. Put it into the oven to get very hot.

3 When hot put the fish on to this and brush with a little melted fat.

4 Cook in a moderately hot oven (400°F.—Gas Mark 5) for 15–25 minutes.

Prawns in tomato sauce

Cooking time   20 minutes

You will need for 1–2 servings:

1–2 dessertspoons thick tomato purée	1 dessertspoon mayonnaise
teaspoon lemon juice	2 oz. prawns
salt	2 oz. rice
sugar	paprika
lemon slices and parsley to garnish	powdered basil
	1 gill white stock or water

1 Season the tomato purée, mix in mayonnaise.

2 Add white stock and prawns.

3 Heat gently in a saucepan.

4 Cook the rice in boiling salted water until tender (for about 20 minutes).

5 Place rice on a hot dish and pour the prawn mixture over it.

6 Garnish with lemon slices and parsley.

Prawn and haddock casserole

Cooking time   10–15 minutes

You will need:

4–6 oz. shelled prawns	1 large smoked haddock, or smoked haddock fillet
½ pint tomato juice (bottled or canned)	
½ oz. flour	pepper
parsley	1 oz. butter

1 Heat the butter in a pan, stir in the flour then add the tomato juice.

2 Bring to the boil and cook until slightly thickened.

3 Cut the haddock into neat pieces, put into the tomato liquid and poach gently for 5 minutes.

4 Add the prawns and cook without boiling for a further 5–10 minutes.

5 Serve with frozen peas and crisp rolls.

6 Decorate with parsley.

Rice and fish ring

Cooking time   20–25 minutes

You will need:

6 oz. rice (preferably Patna rice)	1 can salmon or tuna fish
1–2 oz. grated cheese	2 eggs
1 oz. butter	½ gill milk
1 teaspoon anchovy sauce	seasoning
½ pint white sauce (see page 21)	hard-boiled eggs (optional)

1 Put rice in 3 pints boiling salted water and cook for 15 minutes.

2 Meanwhile make white sauce (see page 21) adding anchovy sauce and flaked salmon.

3 Keep sauce warm while you strain rice.

4 Put rice back in saucepan with beaten eggs, milk, cheese, butter and seasoning. Cook for several minutes until egg is just set.

5 Form into a ring and fill centre with fish mixture.

6 If wished, garnish with sliced hard-boiled egg. *Alternative fillings.* Cooked mushrooms, chopped ham, corned beef, frozen (or canned) prawns and hard-boiled eggs. Mix with sauce as given in recipe above.

Rice and shrimp salad

Cooking time   20 minutes

You will need:

3 oz. rice	2 tablespoons chopped cucumber
1 pint prawns or shrimps	1 tablespoon vinegar
1 tablespoon oil	few capers (not essential)
seasoning	little chopped parsley
to garnish	
lettuce, cress, tomatoes	radishes

1 Cook the rice until just tender in boiling salted water.

2 Strain and mix with the prawns or shrimps and all the other ingredients.

3 Put into a basin or mould and leave until the mixture holds its shape and the rice is quite cold.

4 Turn out on to a bed of lettuce and garnish with sliced tomatoes, cress, water-lilies of radish.

5 Save a few shrimps to put on top of the salad.

Salmon and hard-boiled eggs au gratin

Cooking time   20 minutes

You will need:

1 can concentrated cream of mushroom soup	1 can (small size) pink or red salmon
3 oz. grated cheese	3 or 4 eggs
4 tomatoes	4 slices bread
	parsley and gherkin if wished

1 Put on the eggs to hard-boil, meanwhile heat the soup. Do not dilute it, and add the contents of the tin of salmon.

2 If desired a little chopped parsley and/or chopped gherkin can be added.

3 When the eggs are cooked put into cold water so that they can be shelled easily.

4 Halve the eggs, arrange in a dish, pour the salmon and mushroom mixture on top and cover with grated cheese.

5 Brown under a hot grill.

6 Meanwhile toast the bread and grill the tomatoes.

7 Arrange the tomatoes in a separate dish and cut the toast into triangles.

8 Put these round the edge of the fish dish.

Quick prawn curry

Cooking time   5–10 minutes

You will need:

8 oz. prawns   1 teaspoon curry powder
¼ pint mayonnaise

1 Blend the curry powder with the mayonnaise, add the prawns.

2 To serve cold arrange on a bed of lettuce.

3 To serve hot put into a pan and heat very gently for 5–10 minutes.

Salmon à la Mornay

Cooking time   20 minutes

You will need:

4 cooked potatoes   1 egg yolk
4 oz. grated Swiss   ½ pint white sauce
  cheese   (see page 21)
buttered crumbs   1 can salmon
  (crumbs tossed in
  melted butter)

1 Mash potatoes and line greased baking dish with them.

2 Add cheese and egg yolk to the white sauce and pour half of it over potatoes.

3 Add fish and cover with remaining sauce and buttered breadcrumbs.

4 Bake in a moderate oven for 20 minutes (375°F.—Gas Mark 4).

Quick sauces to serve with fish

White sauce Cooking time   5–8 minutes

| 1 oz. butter or margarine | ½ pint milk for coating consistency i.e. sauce | 1 pint milk for thin white sauce for soups | 1 oz. flour salt. pepper | ¼ pint milk for panada or binding consistency |

1 Heat the butter gently, remove from the heat and stir in the flour.

2 Return to the heat and cook gently for a few minutes, so that the 'roux', as the butter and flour mixture is called, does not brown.

3 Again remove the pan from the heat and gradually blend in the cold milk.

4 Bring to the boil and cook, stirring with a wooden spoon until smooth.

5 Season well. If any small lumps have formed whisk sharply.

Anchovy sauce Cooking time 5 minutes. Make white sauce as in preceding recipe, adding chopped anchovies or 1 teaspoon anchovy essence.

Cheese sauce Cooking time 5–8 minutes. Stir in 3–6 oz. grated cheese when sauce has thickened and add a little mustard.

Lemon sauce No cooking

¼ pint mayonnaise   juice of 1 lemon   grated rind of 1 lemon

Whisk lemon juice into mayonnaise. Add rind.

Shrimp sauce Cooking time 5–8 minutes. Make white sauce, add about ½–1 teacup chopped prawns and a little anchovy essence just before serving. If using fresh prawns simmer shells and use ¼ pint stock instead of the same amount of milk.

Tartare sauce No cooking

| ¼ pint mayonnaise | 2 teaspoons chopped parsley | 2 teaspoons chopped gherkins | 1 teaspoon capers |

Mix all ingredients together.

Scallops and bacon (Escallops)

Cooking time   10 minutes

You will need:

4 scallops   squeeze lemon juice
4 rashers bacon

1 Remove scallops from shells.

2 Add squeeze lemon juice.

3 Wrap round in bacon rashers and put on to a skewer, or on grid of grill pan.

4 Grill steadily until cooked.

5 Take care not to cook too quickly otherwise the bacon will be cooked before scallops.

Scallops in cream sauce (Escallops)

Cooking time   10–12 minutes

You will need:

4 scallops   1 oz. butter
1½ gills milk   1 oz. flour
seasoning   2 tablespoons cream
lemon juice   paprika pepper

1 Simmer the scallops in the milk for 5–6 minutes until just tender.

2 Lift out of the milk and put on to the shells or in a hot dish.

3 Blend flour with the cream, add to the milk together with butter and seasoning.

4 Bring to the boil and cook until smooth and thick. Add squeeze lemon juice.

5 Pour over the scallops. Garnish with red paprika pepper.

6 Serve with rice or toast.

Spiced fish loaf

Cooking time	50 minutes

You will need:

1¼ lb. flaked cooked white fish	3 oz. breadcrumbs
2 eggs	½ gill milk
2 tablespoons chopped gherkins	good grating of nutmeg
	seasoning

1 Mix all the ingredients together.

2 Put into a very well greased loaf tin.

3 Stand this in a tin of water and bake in a very moderate oven (350°F.—Gas Mark 3) for approximately 50 minutes.

4 Serve hot with ¼ pint white sauce poured over the top and arrange olives and sliced egg on top.

Stuffed fillets of fish
(1 helping)

Cooking time	15–20 minutes

You will need:

1 large or 2 small fillets of whiting, plaice or sole	seasoning
margarine	lemon juice (plastic lemons are most practical for you can
tiny jar of lobster, prawn or shrimp paste for stuffing	use a few drops when required and the rest will keep)

1 Wash and dry the fish, season and squeeze a few drops of lemon juice over, spread with the paste.

2 Roll firmly or fold over and put on to a plate with a little margarine.

3 Cover with the saucepan lid or another plate.

4 Stand over a pan of boiling water and cook for 15–20 minutes.

Chapter 4

Poultry and Meat

Poultry and meat cooked in a hurry

When short of time, there is a tendency to feel one must have a succession of grilled or fried meat or poultry. Certainly the more tender pieces of meat cook more quickly—most of them can be grilled and fried in about 15 minutes. However, they do tend to be expensive, and there are many other ways of making quick appetizing meals from more economical ingredients. In the following chapter I have provided you with a variety of new ideas which I trust will give you the basis for a number of new main meals.

With regard to steaks and chops, even these become rather monotonous if always served in the same way. However, with a little imagination and not much extra preparation you can cook your chops and cutlets in many different ways. In fact, if you try some of the recipes in the following pages, you will be able to make the family believe you have spent a long time in preparing them.

Jointed young chicken also lends itself to a variety of tasty recipes, and you will find a number of suggestions for serving it. Boiling chicken can also be delicious and much more economical, as you will see from some of my ideas. For recipes which require longer cooking time, a pressure cooker is a very wise investment for the hurried cook. The pressure cooked recipes which I include in this chapter will be a guide for boiling and stews, and can be varied in a number of ways.

Other quick cooking meats are liver (choose calves' or lambs'), kidneys, bacon and sweetbreads and sausages all of which can be cooked in a number of interesting ways.

Also included are a number of recipes using bacon, gammon and ham, and the latter part of the chapter is devoted to meals made from canned and ready-cooked or frozen meats, all of which can be transformed into quick and satisfying main dishes.

Fried chicken

1 To save time buy the jointed chicken—or if this is not available most shops will cut it up for you. Very small chickens are cut into 2 halves—1 per person; larger ones into 4 joints (2 leg joints—2 breast and wing).

2 For quicker frying deep fat is advisable, and one should allow 5–6 minutes at a fairly high heat then turn the heat down for further 10–15 minutes.

Either coat with egg and crumbs or with seasoned flour or batter.

3 For shallow frying do NOT use batter, but seasoned flour or egg and crumbs, and fry steadily in hot butter for 15–20 minutes. If preferred the chicken can be browned only in the fat then transferred to a moderately hot oven and roasted for 25 minutes.

4 Serve with: Fried vegetables and salad. Fried bananas and canned or frozen corn.

Grilled chicken

This takes about the same time as frying. The poultry should be well brushed with plenty of hot butter.

Serve with grilled bacon, tomatoes, or tomato sauce (see page 38).

Mushrooms and grilled chicken

Cooking time   15–25 minutes

You will need:

very young chicken, jointed (either 1 large or 2 small)	8 oz. mushrooms
	4 chopped shallots
	1 crushed clove garlic
3 oz. butter	1 tablespoon chopped
breadcrumbs	parsley

1 Heat butter in grill pan.

2 Add to that the thinly sliced mushrooms, the shallots, the garlic and the parsley.

3 Joint very young chicken—use 1 large or 2 smaller birds and brush the chickens with melted butter, cook in the grill pan, on top of the mushrooms, etc., turning frequently.

4 Just before serving, sprinkle each joint with breadcrumbs. Replace under grill and brown.

Chicken country style

Cooking time   35–40 minutes

You will need:

4 joints frying chicken	2 oz. butter
½ can milk	can concentrated vege-
2 tablespoons chopped parsley	table soup
	1 clove garlic (can be omitted) seasoning

1 Brown joints of chicken in hot butter in pan with crushed garlic.

2 Add vegetable soup.

3 Pour enough milk into can to half fill, then pour this into saucepan.

4 Stir well until soup has dissolved.

5 Bring to boil and simmer until tender. Season well.

6 Serve garnished with parsley.

Chicken biscaienne

Cooking time   30 minutes

You will need:

small young chicken	1 or 2 leaves of sage
2 oz. bacon (green bacon being best)	1 oz. butter
	1 small onion
1 oz. flour	5 tomatoes
	salt and pepper

1 Cut up the chicken into pieces for serving.

2 Fry these for 1–2 minutes with the chopped bacon.

3 Add butter.

4 Sprinkle with flour, stir well and add chopped onion.

5 Cook on for 2 or 3 minutes, then add peeled tomatoes and sage.

6 Season well with salt and pepper, put on the lid and cook gently for about 25 minutes, shaking the pan now and again.

Economical chicken pie

Cooking time   35 minutes

You will need:

8 oz. shortcrust pastry (see page 86)

filling

1 can condensed cream of chicken soup or ½ pint **thick** chicken stock	salt
	pepper
	1 teaspoon lemon juice
4 oz. cooked chicken (diced)	1 hard-boiled egg

to glaze a little milk

1 Line an 8-inch flan ring or sandwich tin with ⅔ of the pastry.

2 Mix the cream of chicken soup with cooked chicken, seasoning and lemon juice.

3 Spread the mixture in pastry case.

4 Arrange sliced hard-boiled egg on top.

5 Cover with remaining pastry, seal edges and flute.

6 Brush with milk and bake in a moderately hot oven (400°F.—Gas Mark 5) for 30–35 minutes.

7 Serve hot with vegetables or cold with salad.

Corn and chicken platter

Cooking time   10 minutes

You will need for 2–3 servings

1–5oz. packet quick-frozen sweet corn*	8 oz. cooked diced chicken
for the dressing	
4 tablespoons oil	1 tablespoon vinegar
salt, pepper	sugar, salt
olives	chopped parsley

* Canned corn needs no cooking.

1 Cook the sweet corn according to directions on the packet and leave to get cold.
2 Marinade the chicken in the French dressing for about 1 hour.
3 Arrange on a dish with the sweet corn and garnish with olives and parsley.

Snacks with chicken left-overs

1
Stuff tomatoes with tiny untidy pieces of chicken chopped very finely and mixed with diced cucumber and mayonnaise.

2
Combine .the pieces of chicken with a thick sauce.

3
Mix the chicken with scrambled egg as a filling for pastry cases, in sandwiches or on toast.

USING A BOILING CHICKEN WISELY

A boiling chicken is an excellent buy for you can use it in so many different dishes. For example:

Meal No. **1** (hot)

Chicken with Egg Sauce   Slice the breast from the boiled chicken, then serve on rice or with vegetables with a hard-boiled egg sauce i.e. add chopped hard-boiled egg white to white sauce (see page 21, but make with half chicken stock and half milk). Garnish with crisp bacon rolls and the egg yolk and mixed vegetables.

Meal No. **2**

Chicken Royal   Another hot meal. Dice the meat from 1 leg and thigh. Add a wing if not enough. Make up $\frac{3}{4}$ pint white sauce—or to save even more time make up extra sauce and save $\frac{3}{4}$ pint from first dish. Add the diced chicken, a chopped pepper, the corn from a corn on the cob (gently cooked), 1 chopped slice of ham. Serve on buttered toast or with vegetables.

Meal No. **3** (cold)

Chicken mould   Make 1 pint tomato flavoured jelly by dissolving $\frac{3}{4}$ oz. powder gelatine in 1 pint tomato juice (buy the tomato juice that hasn't a lot of Worcester). When cold, but not set, add 2 teacups diced cooked chicken, chopped hard-boiled egg, cup mixed vegetables. Pour into a mould and allow to set. Serve with salad.

Mixed grill

cooking time   10–30 minutes

The ingredients can vary but choose a selection of the following:

You will need:

a small cutlet	sausage
piece of steak	piece of lambs' or
lamb or pigs' kidney	calves' liver
mushrooms	halved or whole tomatoes
rasher of bacon	

1 Put the mushrooms and tomatoes in the grill pan, seasoning well.
2 Start these under a hot grill for a few minutes.
3 Put the meat (well seasoned), with the exception of the bacon, on the grid, brushing with plenty of melted butter, margarine or fat.
4 Cook quickly, turning as necessary.
5 Add bacon at the last minute so this will not be overcooked.
6 Arrange on hot dish and serve with peas, French fried potatoes, chipped or sauté potatoes.
7 Accompany with a crisp green salad if wished.

Grilled steak

Cooking time   5–15 minutes

1 Brush grid and steak with butter or olive oil.
2 Season steak and if wished break down tissues by 'banging' with rolling pin or meat tenderiser. Or you may care to marinade the meat by leaving it to stand for 1 hour in a mixture of oil and vinegar to which you add seasoning,

including a pinch garlic salt or crushed clove garlic.

3 Put on to grid of grill pan with tomatoes, mushrooms at bottom of pan.

4 Cook rapidly on either side under hot grill for a few minutes.

5 This is sufficient for people who like their steak 'rare' (underdone) in the centre, but if you like it well done, lower the heat and cook steadily.

6 Garnish with watercress, parsley butter (see page 19) perhaps adding a dash Worcester sauce instead of lemon, asparagus tips, fried onion rings, croûtons of bread.

7 Serve with mixed vegetables, potatoes, and try a really crisp salad with French dressing as an accompaniment.

The most popular steaks for grilling are:

Rump
An excellent flavour, a little less tender than steaks from fillet.

Fillet
Particularly tender. The fillet is limited so this is expensive, for it comes from the undercut of sirloin.

Minute
A thin steak, generally cut from fillet, which needs only $\frac{1}{2}$–1 minute's cooking on either side.

Sirloin
A steak cut from the sirloin, not undercut, excellent flavour.

Porterhouse
Large piece of sirloin steak.

Chateaubriand
A very large fillet steak.

To fry steak

Cooking time   3–12 minutes

Choose same quality and cuts of steak as for grilling.

1 Heat a good knob of butter or olive oil in the pan and put in the steak.

2 Brown quickly on either side to seal in the flavour.

3 Lower the heat and cook gently for about 10–12 minutes for well done steak—about 6–8 minutes for medium cooked and 3–4 for underdone.

4 French or English mustard are the usual accompaniment. Some people like Worcester sauce. Tomatoes, mushrooms, watercress are the best garnish, or fried onion rings.

To fry onions

Cooking time   8 minutes

1 Peel and cut onions into rings.

2 Separate rings. Dip in milk and seasoned flour.

3 Shake off surplus flour and fry in shallow or deep fat.

Tournedos of steak

Buy fillet steaks and ask the butcher to tie them into rounds to form tournedos. If you prefer to use small wooden or metal skewers you can do so. To keep outer side of meat very moist wrap fat bacon around it. Fry or grill as preferred. Serve on rounds of fried bread.

Tournedos of
Steak Africaine

Grill or fry the steaks. Garnish with fried banana. Serve with horseradish sauce.

Tournedos of
Steak Artésienne

Fry the steak. Garnish with rounds of aubergine, tomatoes and/or celery. Top with rings of fried onion.

Tournedos of
Steak Belle-Hélène

Fry the steak, garnish with asparagus and truffle. Truffles are obtained in cans and are very expensive, so mushrooms can be substituted.

Fillet steaks
à l'Américaine

Cooking time   10–15 minutes
You will need:

4 fillet steaks	1 egg
crisp breadcrumbs	4 bananas
creamed potatoes or	watercress
potato crisps	horseradish sauce

1 Peel and halve the bananas, dip them in beaten egg and roll in breadcrumbs.

2 Fry in a little butter.

3 Serve on top of the grilled fillet steaks.

4 Arrange on a hot dish with a border of piped potatoes or potato crisps and pour a little of the sauce round.

To make the horseradish sauce: Stir either 2 tablespoons fresh, grated horseradish or 2 tablespoons bottled horseradish into $\frac{1}{2}$ pint creamy white sauce (see page 21). Add a little extra seasoning.

Steak Diane

Cooking time   3–4 minutes

1 Fry minute steaks (very thin steaks) in hot butter.
2 A little finely chopped shallot and parsley together with a few drops of Worcester sauce or brandy can be added to the butter before putting in the meat.
3 Serve at once.

Casserole of steak

Cooking time   15–20 minutes

You will need:

4 small fillet steaks	can vegetable soup
pinch herbs	water
slice bread	salt
pepper	made mustard

1 Heat soup and approximately $\frac{1}{2}$ pint water in pan.
2 Put in steaks, herbs, salt and pepper.
3 Simmer gently for 10–15 minutes.
4 Spread a small slice crustless bread with mustard and cook for 5 minutes.
5 Beat into liquid so bread disintegrates to thicken sauce.

Speedy beef stroganoff

Cooking time   10 minutes

You will need:

1 large onion	pinch pepper
1 can button mushrooms, drained	$\frac{1}{2}$ teaspoon salt
1 lb. rump or fillet steak	$\frac{1}{8}$ teaspoon garlic salt
$\frac{1}{2}$–1 teaspoon paprika	1 teaspoon diced parsley
$\frac{1}{4}$ pint sour cream*	4 oz. cooked rice or noodles

or thin cream and 1 tablespoon lemon juice

1 Sauté onion and mushrooms in butter or margarine very gently until onion is tender.
2 Add steak and cook very gently, stirring constantly, for about 5 minutes.
3 The meat should not brown and should be rare inside.
4 Add the pepper, salt, garlic salt, parsley and paprika.
5 Stir and simmer for 3 or 4 minutes longer.
6 Just before serving add the sour cream.
7 Heat briefly, serve over rice or noodles.

Hamburgers de luxe

Cooking time   10 12 minutes

You will need:

1 lb. minced rump steak	good pinch herbs
4 oz. soft crumbs	soft rolls

1 tablespoon chopped onion	seasoning
	1 egg

1 Make the patties by mixing meat, crumbs, onion, seasoning, herbs and egg together.
2 Form into 8 flat cakes.
3 Fry carefully on both sides.
4 If wished add a slice of cheese on top just before serving between the rolls.
5 Serve as well big bowls of crisp lettuce, chicory, watercress and quartered fresh tomatoes.
6 Have fresh fruit salad, or cheese and crust bread to follow.

Cheeseburger

Cooking time   10 minutes

You will need:

hamburger mixture

1$\frac{1}{2}$ oz. breadcrumbs	6–8 oz. fairly lean steak, minced
1 tablespoon minced or grated onion	pinch pepper and salt
$\frac{1}{2}$ egg to bind.	

cheese rarebit mixture

1 oz. butter or margarine	pinch salt and cayenne pepper
1 level teaspoon made mustard	6 oz. grated Cheddar cheese
4 hamburger buns or soft rolls	2 tablespoons milk

1 Make the hamburgers.
2 Mix together all the ingredients, divide into equal portions and shape into round flat cakes slightly larger than the buns.
3 Prepare the rarebit mixture.
4 Cream the butter or margarine with the seasonings, add grated cheese and milk and mix well.
5 Grill or fry the hamburgers 2 or 3 minutes on each side.
6 Spread a generous helping of the rarebit mixture over both sides of each split hamburger bun and grill to a golden brown.
7 Put a cooked hamburger on bottom of the grilled bun and close.
8 Serve hot with mustard or ketchup.

Beefburgers on baps

Cooking time   10 minutes

You will need for 10–12 beefburgers:

1$\frac{1}{2}$ lb. finely minced beefsteak	1 heaped tablespoon browned breadcrumbs
$\frac{1}{4}$ teaspoon black pepper	2 teaspoons made mustard
1 medium onion, in wafer-thin slices	2 tomatoes, sliced
1 teaspoon salt	5 or 6 bap rolls
	little butter

1 Blend the minced meat, salt, pepper and mustard and shape into 10–12 flat cakes.

2 Place in grill pan, without the grid, and grill at medium heat for 5 minutes each side, or less if preferred rare.

3 Halve, toast and butter the bap rolls; top each with a beefburger and top these with a wafer slice of onion, slice of tomato and a sprinkle of crumbs.

4 Dot the top of each with butter and slip under the hot grill for about 3 minutes.

Viennese steaks

Cooking time   15 minutes

You will need for 6 servings

1–2 tablespoons tomato ketchup	½ level teaspoon finely crushed dried mixed herbs
1½–2 lb minced beef	
1 dessertspoon chopped parsley	2 eggs
little grated nutmeg	1 or 2 onions
black pepper	flour
salt	butter or oil for frying
	brown sauce (see page 37)

1 Mix the minced meat with parsley, nutmeg, seasonings and mixed herbs to taste.

2 Separate 1 egg and set white aside.

3 Beat yolk with another whole egg and use to bind meat mixture.

4 Divide into portions and shape each with floured hands to look like rather large slices of fillet steak.

5 Dredge with flour on all sides.

6 Fry in heated butter or oil until well browned on both sides, then drain and keep hot.

7 Peel and slice onion.

8 Coat with flour, dip into beaten white of egg, then into flour again, and fry until golden and crisp.

9 Serve as a garnish. Or cook a larger quantity and serve round the steaks.

10 Serve brown sauce separately.

Goulash

Pressure cooking time   20–25 minutes

You will need:

1 lb. stewing meat (preferably beef)	1 oz. fat
1 onion	1 gill tomato pulp
seasoning (include 1–2 teaspoons paprika pepper)	1 lb. potatoes
	¼ pint stock or water

1 Cut the meat into neat cubes.

2 Heat the fat at the bottom of the cooker and fry the meat and onion until brown.

3 Add the tomato pulp, stock, seasoning and paprika.

4 Fix the lid and bring to pressure.

5 Lower heat and cook for a good 10 minutes.

6 Allow pressure to drop then add the sliced potatoes.

7 Re-fix the lid, bring once again to pressure, lower the heat and cook for 10 minutes.

8 This should be a very thick stew.

Braised heart

Pressure cooking time   25 minutes

You will need:

1 lb. either ox heart or sheep heart	1 oz. flour
	1 oz. dripping
bunch herbs or 1 teaspoon mixed herbs	2 onions
	2 carrots
½ pint stock or water flavoured with meat or vegetable extract	1 small turnip
	seasoning

1 Cut the ox heart into thick slices.

2 Heat the fat in the bottom of the pressure cooker.

3 Flour the hearts and season well.

4 Fry in the hot fat until brown.

5 Add all the other ingredients except the 1 oz. flour.

6 Fix the lid and bring to pressure.

7 Lower the heat and cook for 25 minutes, allow pressure to drop.

8 Blend flour with a very little cold stock, add to the liquid. Bring to the boil and boil for 3 minutes.

Boiled brisket

Pressure cooking time   25–30 minutes

You will need for 6 servings:

2 lb. brisket of beef*	½ pint water
2 large carrots	seasoning
2 onions	bunch of parsley
1 small turnip	

1 Cut the vegetables into fairly large pieces.

2 Put into the cooker with the meat, parsley, seasoning and water.

3 Fix the lid and bring to pressure.

4 Lower the heat and cook for 25 minutes.

5 Allow pressure to drop gradually.

6 Boiled beef is served with unthickened gravy.
Note: If the meat is salted, soak for a good hour before cooking. Instead of brisket, top-side or silverside of beef can be used.

Brisket salad

Cooked brisket is excellent served cold.
If cooking at home (see preceding recipe) allow to cool in the liquid.
If serving hot, first carve off required amount, then return meat to liquid.
Arrange on a bed of green salad and serve with pickles and mayonnaise.

Liver, fried or grilled

Cooking time   4–8 minutes

When frying or grilling liver, do remember that it should never be overcooked, otherwise instead of being moist and tender it becomes hard and dry. Coat with very little seasoned flour and fry with bacon or brush with melted butter and grill. Allow 2–4 minutes either side depending on thickness.

Devilled liver

Cooking time   6–10 minutes
You will need:

1 lb. calves' liver cut in thin slices	2 oz. margarine or butter
2 teaspoons chutney	1 teaspoon curry powder
salt	2 oz. breadcrumbs
pepper	1 teaspoon Worcester sauce
bacon	pinch of cayenne pepper
toast	tomatoes

1 Cream margarine with other ingredients and spread on both sides of slices of liver.
2 Heat the grill for a few minutes, put liver under this and cook for 3 minutes.
3 Turn liver over, arrange seasoned, halved tomatoes and rolled rashers of bacon round it.
4 Grill for a further 3 minutes.
5 If liver is thick, lower heat and cook for several more minutes.
6 Arrange liver, bacon and tomatoes on hot dish with triangles of toast.

Liver pancakes

Cooking time   15–20 minutes
You will need:

basic pancake mixture (see page 73)	6 oz. calves' liver
1 large onion	2 oz. butter or fat
2 or 3 mushrooms	2 large skinned tomatoes
	butter or fat for cooking

to garnish

fried tomatoes	little parsley
fried mushrooms	

1 Make pancake mixture, season it extra well.
2 Chop the liver finely, slice the onion very thinly and the tomatoes fairly thickly.
3 Heat the butter or fat and cook the onion, then the tomatoes, then add the liver and cook gently for about 4 or 5 minutes—or more.
4 Lastly add the finely chopped mushrooms and cook for a further 1 or 2 minutes.
5 Cook the pancakes and fill with the liver mixture.
6 Roll firmly and put on to a hot dish.
7 Meanwhile, fry mushrooms, tomatoes and parsley for garnish.
8 Serve pancakes with garnish and a good brown gravy.

9 Cooked minced meat can be used in the same way.

Liver casserole

Cooking time   20 minutes
You will need:

12 oz. calves' or lambs liver*	packet frozen mixed vegetables
1½ oz. butter or margarine	just under ½ pint stock or water
1 oz. flour	seasoning
1 small chopped or grated onion	

* Ox liver could be used but will need about 1½ hours cooking or 15 minutes in pressure cooker.

1 Cut liver into fingers and coat with seasoned flour.
2 Fry in hot butter with the onion for 2 minutes on either side.
3 Add liquid and seasoning.
4 Bring to boil and cook until thickened.
5 Add frozen vegetables and cook for about 10 minutes.
6 Serve with creamed potatoes or rice.

Sweetbreads en brochette

Cooking time   30 minutes

1 Sweetbreads can be served in the same way as lamb en brochette (see page 29).
2 Boil steadily in salted water until nearly tender. Strain, remove skin and gristle, cut into neat pieces.
3 Put a small roll of bacon, a piece of sweetbread, a small roll of bacon on the skewer and continue like this until the skewer is filled.
4 Season and cook until tender.
5 Serve with crisp toast.

To fry or grill lamb

Cooking time   12–15 minutes

Choose loin or best end of neck chops or cutlets.

1 Since lamb contains a reasonable amount of fat no extra fat need be added when frying or grilling.
2 Have the grill hot to begin with, and brown the meat on either side then lower to moderate to cook through to the centre.
3 Fry the chops or cutlets steadily rather than too quickly to give a pleasant crispness to the outside fat of lamb.
4 Serve with grilled or fried tomatoes—mushrooms—or with tomato sauce (see page 38). *Note:* Generally speaking, mutton is not suitable for grilling or frying and even if tender will take considerably more time than lamb.

Lamb cutlets in mint jelly

Cooking time   10–15 minutes

You will need:

4 lightly grilled lamb cutlets—it will save time if you roast a loin of lamb and cut off 4 cutlets from this
seasoning
$\frac{3}{4}$ gill water
sugar
cooked peas
mayonnaise
1 teaspoon powder gelatine

1 tablespoon lemon juice (use the juice from a plastic lemon, if wished) OR
1 tablespoon vinegar
1 tablespoon chopped mint
cooked potatoes
chopped parsley

1 Put the cutlets into a shallow dish.
2 Dissolve the gelatine in the very hot water, then stir in the lemon juice or vinegar, seasoning and mint.
3 Add little sugar to taste.
4 Pour over the cutlets and allow to set.
5 Arrange the cooked potatoes, tossed in mayonnaise and chopped parsley, and the cooked peas round the edge of the dish.
6 The chops or cutlets keep beautifully moist covered with the mint mixture, so you can prepare this dish for the family well ahead, and they can help themselves.

Lamb en brochette

Cooking time   10 minutes

You will need:

several thick slices lamb from leg or shoulder
cocktail sausages
grilled tomatoes

$\frac{1}{2}$ lambs' or pigs' kidney (optional)
melted butter
crumbs
rice

1 Cut into neat squares of about 1 inch.
2 Put on a skewer together with sausages and lambs' or pigs' kidney.
3 Brush with melted butter, season and roll in crumbs.
4 Cook under the grill.
5 Serve still on the skewers, on a bed of rice, garnished with grilled tomatoes. French mustard should accompany this.

Grilled lamb cutlets with forcemeat stuffing

Cooking time   15 minutes

You will need:

4 lamb cutlets or lamb chops
for the stuffing
2 large or 4 small skinned sausages OR
4 oz. sausage meat
teaspoon grated lemon rind

1 egg yolk
2 teaspoons chopped parsley
pinch mixed herbs
seasoning

1 Mix ingredients for stuffing together.
2 Cut the meat away from the bone for 2–3 inches.
3 Press stuffing in the cavity making it flat and neat.
4 Put the stuffed chops under grill.
5 Cook on both sides until crisp and brown.
6 Serve with potato crisps, grilled tomatoes, peas and watercress.

Devilled lamb

Cooking time   15 minutes

You will need:

4 lamb chops
1 tablespoon chopped parsley
1 teaspoon Worcester sauce

2 oz. butter
pinch curry powder

1 Put chops under hot grill and brown well on one side.
2 Turn and cook on second side for 1 minute.
3 Blend butter, parsley, sauce and curry powder.
4 Spread over hot chops and cook steadily for about 8 minutes under grill.

Quick lamb hotpot

Cooking time   30 minutes

You will need:

4 lamb chops
$\frac{3}{4}$ pint water
1 small onion or little diced onion

1 beef bouillon cube
packet frozen vegetables
seasoning
caper sauce (see page 37)

1 Put water and bouillon cube into saucepan.
2 Add chopped or dried onion and lamb chops, season well.
3 Simmer gently for 20 minutes.
4 Add vegetables and cook for further 10 minutes. Make caper sauce using a little of the stock as well as milk.
5 Lift lamb and vegetables on to hot dish and serve with sauce.

Tomato lamb hotpot

As in preceding recipe but instead of water and bouillon cube use 1 can tomato soup and $\frac{1}{4}$ pint water. Serve with rice or cooked spaghetti.

Fried and grilled kidneys

Cooking time   10 minutes

Pigs' or lambs' kidneys are best for frying or grilling.

To fry

1 Halve kidneys, remove gristle.
2 Toss the meat in seasoned flour.
3 Fry steadily in hot margarine or butter.

4 Serve with toast, fried bacon and vegetables.

To grill

1 Prepare as for frying, except the kidneys need no flouring.
2 Brush with plenty of melted butter.
3 Grill steadily.
4 Serve with grilled mushrooms, tomatoes, etc.
Note. Allow 1–2 kidneys per person.

Kebabs

Cooking time   10–15 minutes

You will need:

4 lambs' kidneys	4 sausages
4 small mushrooms	2 rashers of bacon
little flour	seasoning
cooked rice	stock or thin soup

1 Halve the kidneys and sausages and rashers of bacon, dust lightly with seasoned flour.
2 Put the meat etc., and the mushrooms on to 4 skewers.
3 Leave these all ready, then all the family need do is to put them under a hot grill, turning once or twice until the kidneys are tender.
4 If wished have rice cooked in a double saucepan, so it does not burn. Moisten this with a little stock or thin soup, and it will keep hot to serve with the kebabs. Put kebabs on to a bed of crisp watercress.

Kidneys in port wine sauce

Cooking time   15 minutes

You will need for 3–4 servings:

6–8 lambs' kidneys	1 oz. flour
2 oz. butter	seasoning
¼ pint water or stock	¼ pint port wine
little chopped onion	pinch mixed herbs
(can be omitted)	

1 Cut each kidney into 4, removing gristle.
2 Toss in the seasoned flour.
3 Fry gently with the onion in the butter for 5 minutes.
4 Add stock, port wine, herbs, seasoning.
5 Bring to boil and cook until thickened.
6 Simmer for further 5 minutes.
7 Serve with rice, creamed potatoes or toast.

Kidneys and scrambled egg

Cooking time   12 minutes

You will need:

2 lambs' kidneys	2 oz. butter
seasoning	4 slices fried bread or
4 eggs	buttered toast

1 Cut the kidneys into small pieces, season well.
2 Heat butter and cook kidneys in this for about 7–8 minutes, if necessary add a tablespoon water to prevent sticking.

3 Beat and season eggs lightly, add to kidney and continue cooking until firm.
4 Serve on toast or fried bread.

To fry and grill pork

Choose loin chops or cutlets for either frying or grilling. Cutlets should have the bone trimmed to look more attractive when served.

To fry

1 Brown chops on both sides lightly in the pan then lower the heat and cook steadily through to the centre.
2 Pork should be fried steadily so that you draw the fat from the meat and no extra fat is then required.

To grill

1 Make sure grill is hot before starting to cook pork chops.
2 Pork chops or cutlets need little basting with fat, since there is generally a good distribution of fat and lean.
3 When once the outside of the meat has been sealed turn the heat low to make sure they are well cooked through to the centre.
4 Serve with fried apple rings or sauce and orange salad or just with grilled tomatoes, mushrooms.

Grilled pork chops with orange slices

Cooking time   15 minutes

1 Season pork chops and brown on either side under hot grill.
2 Add thick slices of orange sprinkled with a little brown sugar and cook together until the chops are tender and the orange slices hot.
3 Serve with watercress, peas and creamed potatoes.

Barbecued pork

Cooking time   35–40 minutes

You will need:

4 pork chops	2 onions
4 tomatoes	2 eating apples
1 oz. fat	seasoning
½ gill	

1 Slice onions very thinly.
2 Fry in the fat until fairly soft, using large pan or frying pan.
3 Add water, the thickly sliced tomatoes. Arrange chops on top and season well.
4 Core, but do not peel the apples. Slice and arrange on top of the chops.

5 Put lid on pan or plate over frying pan and cook steadily, adding little extra water if necessary.

Grilled gammon rashers

Cooking time   10 minutes

1 Grilled gammon or grilled thick back bacon rashers (bacon chops) are delicious served with tomatoes, mushrooms, etc., and try grilling eggs in the pan underneath. Heat a little fat in grill pan, drop in eggs, put bacon on the grid and cook together.
Or try:
2 Grilling thick gammon rashers and when nearly cooked, put rings of pineapple, brushed with a little melted butter under the grill.
3 Serve together with watercress.

Gammon and cheese with Lyonnaise potatoes

Cooking time   25 minutes

You will need:

about 1 lb. sliced cooked potatoes	8–12 oz. thinly sliced onions
4 thick slices gammon	4 slices cheese
lettuce	little margarine
tomatoes	

1 Put margarine into a pan and heat.
2 Fry the onions in pan until nearly soft, mixed with sliced, cooked potatoes.
3 Put lid on frying pan and cook very gently until potatoes are very hot and golden brown and onions tender.
4 Meanwhile fry or grill thick gammon rashers.
5 Just before serving put a slice of cheese on each rasher of bacon and melt under grill. Or put the slices of cheese in the frying pan and when just melting lift on to bacon.
6 Serve with a dish of sliced raw tomatoes and crisp lettuce in addition to the potatoes.

Gammon rashers with Vinaigrette Beans

Cooking time   10–15 minutes

You will need:

4 gammon rashers	packet frozen beans or canned beans or 1 lb. fresh French beans
1 egg	
1 tablespoon chutney	
seasoning	1 tablespoon chopped parsley
1 teaspoon vinegar	
2 tablespoons breadcrumbs	1 oz. butter (or use gammon fat)

1 Score the fat of the gammon rashers and put under the grill when not too hot (or cook in a frying pan).

2 By putting the bacon under a moderate grill you prevent the edges curling.
3 Meanwhile, either cook the frozen or fresh beans or heat the canned beans.
4 While bacon and beans are cooking, hard-boil and chop the egg.
5 Drain the beans and melt the butter in the pan, or use the bacon fat.
6 Toss the breadcrumbs in this, add parsley, chopped egg, chutney, vinegar.
7 Arrange gammon rashers on a dish surrounded by beans.
8 Garnish with the egg mixture.

Bacon and mushroom casserole

Cooking time   10–15 minutes

You will need:

6 oz. quick-cooking macaroni	4–6 oz. grated cheese
	4 rashers streaky bacon
1 onion (could be omitted)	1 can concentrated mushroom soup
1 oz. butter	seasoning

1 Put the macaroni into boiling salted water, bring water to boil again for 7 minutes, making sure it is cooking fairly quickly.
2 Meanwhile dice and fry the onion in the butter, then add the diced bacon and fry this.
3 Add the concentrated mushroom soup, heat thoroughly.
4 Strain the macaroni, tip into a large hot dish, cover with the mushroom mixture and the cheese and brown under a very hot grill.
Variations: Use kidney soup instead of mushroom. Add can of crabmeat instead of bacon. Add can of tuna fish instead of bacon. Use tomato instead of the mushroom soup.

Bacon pancakes

Cooking time   25 minutes

You will need:

for the batter

4 oz. flour	pinch salt
½ pint milk and water	1 egg

for the filling

4–6 oz. streaky bacon	1 small onion
2 oz. mushrooms	2 or 3 large tomatoes
little extra fat for cooking the filling and the pancakes	parsley to garnish
	cheese or tomato sauce

1 Make the batter by mixing the flour (sieved with the salt) with the egg and enough liquid to make a stiff batter.
2 Beat well until smooth then add the rest of the liquid.
3 Allow to stand.
4 Meanwhile prepare the filling.
5 Remove the bacon rinds and fry these to obtain the fat from them, lift the rinds from

the pan, add a little extra fat if necessary and fry the onion (finely chopped) then the bacon. chopped mushrooms and tomatoes.

6 Keep this hot and season well.

7 Cook the pancakes.

8 Fill each and roll firmly, or if preferred put 1 pancake on a hot dish, spread with the filling, cover with a pancake and so on until all are used.

9 Serve with cheese sauce or a tomato sauce (see pages 21, 38) and garnish with parsley.

Sausages   *in sweet-sour sauce*

Cooking time   20 minutes

You will need:

1 lb. sausages
4 oz. spaghetti (macaroni, rice or noodles may be used instead)

for sauce

½ pint cider	1–2 oz. chopped celery or
little salt	chopped green pepper
pepper	4 sliced tomatoes
1–2 tablespoons capers	1 good tablespoon sugar

1 Put sauce ingredients in pan and simmer for about 20 minutes.

2 Meanwhile fry or grill sausages and cook spaghetti in boiling salted water for 7–10 minutes (some spaghetti will take longer to cook than this).

3 Drain spaghetti and arrange on hot dish.

4 Arrange sausages round like spokes of a wheel, pour sauce in centre.

Sausages   *with barbecue sauce*

Cooking time   10–15 minutes

You will need for 4–6 servings

12 sausages (or better still 12 Frankfurter sausages)	little cream cheese
	1 loaf of bread
	radishes

for the sauce*

4 tablespoons tomato ketchup or tomato chutney	2 teaspoons made mustard (French or English)
shake of pepper and salt	1 teaspoon sugar

*If wished, a little Worcester sauce can also be added to the tomato sauce mixture.

1 Cook the sausages until brown and tender. Frankfurter sausages need no cooking, but can be brushed with melted margarine and browned to look more attractive.

2 Cut slices of bread and arrange these with the sausages on a large dish or plate.

3 Blend all the ingredients for the sauce together and transfer this to a small dish in the centre of the plate.

4 Cut the radishes into the shape of flowers. Allow them to stand in cold water for several hours so the 'petals' open out.

5 Press a little soft cream cheese into the centre of each flower and put these on the same platter.

6 Everyone can just help themselves to bread and sausage and dip the sausages into the spicy, tomato flavoured sauce.

Sausage jambalaya

Cooking time   25 minutes

You will need:

6 oz. Patna rice	1 clove of garlic
1 large onion	8 oz. or can tomatoes
seasoning	pinch cayenne pepper
2–3 oz. butter or margarine for frying	1 finely chopped red or green pepper when in
1 lb. chipolata sausages	season

1 Fry the sausages in a pan, then lift out and fry the finely chopped onion and garlic.

2 Add the tomatoes and pepper, simmer until soft.

3 Put the rice into a pan of boiling salted water and cook until just tender.

4 Strain, add to the onion mixture.

5 Season well, add the sausages, and if using fresh tomatoes stir in a little stock to keep the mixture moist.

Grilled frankfurters   *on toast*

Cooking time   5–8 minutes

1 Brush Frankfurters with little margarine.

2 Put under grill allowing 2 Frankfurters and ¼ rasher of bacon per person.

3 Serve with hot buttered toast spread lightly with mustard.

To fry or grill veal

Chops from loin or best end of neck, or fillets (thin slices cut from leg) are ideal for either frying or grilling.

To fry

1 If wished, coat with egg and crumbs, or flour. This helps to keep flavour of meat.

2 Keep moistened with plenty of fat while frying.

3 Fry steadily until tender and golden brown.

To grill

1 Brush with plenty of melted butter and margarine to prevent drying.

2 Grill steadily until done and serve with grilled bacon.

Escallopes of veal

Cooking time   10 minutes

Buy thin slices (cut from the leg), beat gently with rolling pin to flatten even more.

2 Fry steadily in shallow fat, oil or butter and oil mixed, until golden brown on both sides.

3 Garnish with wedges of lemon or, for a more elaborate garnish, top rings of lemon with freshly chopped hard-boiled egg and parsley, or egg and capers. Excellent with green salad.

Fillets of veal
in cream sauce

Cooking time   10 minutes

1 Use thin slices of veal but do not coat with egg and crumbs.

2 Season and fry gently in hot butter or margarine until tender.

3 Lift on to hot dish.

4 Add small amount of cream to the butter left in pan.

5 Heat gently and pour over veal.

Swiss veal foldovers

Cooking time   30 minutes

You will need:

4 veal fillets	rice
4 slices processed Swiss cheese	¼ teaspoon paprika
	2 oz. fat
1 can condensed cream of mushroom soup	½ pint light cream
	½ gill cooking Sauternes
4 squares boiled ham	2 tablespoons flour

1 Pound each veal slice to a very thin rectangle (about 8 x 4 inches).

2 Cut cheese and ham slices in half.

3 Stack alternately in centre of each veal fillet.

4 Fold veal over to cover cheese and ham, roll carefully in mixture of flour and paprika.

5 Brown in hot fat.

6 Mix remaining ingredients, add to pan.

7 Cover, simmer, stirring occasionally, 30 minutes or till tender.

8 Serve with hot rice.

Veal rolls

Cooking time   30 minutes

You will need:

4 fillets veal	seasoning
4 fingers Gruyère or Cheddar cheese	1 can concentrated tomato soup
4 small pieces cooked ham	water

1 Put the ham and cheese on the seasoned fillets veal.

2 Roll firmly and skewer or tie.

3 Put soup and an equal amount of water into pan.

4 Bring to the boil, stir until smooth.

5 Simmer veal rolls in the liquid for 25 minutes.

6 Instead of cheese and ham the meat can be filled with stuffing and chopped fried mushrooms.

Paprika veal

Cooking time   about 40 minutes

You will need for one serving:

1 veal chop	1 teaspoon paprika pepper
potatoes	
tiny knob of margarine	1 can peas or small packet frozen peas if wished
seasoning	
1 can tomatoes (small size)	½ gill water

1 Heat the margarine and fry the veal chop in this for a minute or so on both sides.

2 Open the can of tomatoes, add to the meat, together with the paprika pepper, blended with water.

3 Add the halved potatoes and seasoning and simmer steadily for about 30 minutes until the potatoes are tender.

4 You should have a tightly fitting lid for this.

5 Add the well-drained peas (or the frozen peas), and replace the lid.

6 Watch the liquid the first time you make this, as it might evaporate too quickly, and you will need to add just a little extra water. It should, however, be a thick mixture.

Veal milanaise

Cooking time   20 minutes

You will need:

4 veal chops	1 can spaghetti in tomato sauce
4 skinned tomatoes	
seasoning	few capers
2 oz. butter	

1 Fry chops in the butter for 15 minutes.

2 Put on to hot dish.

3 Add sliced tomatoes and spaghetti to fat in pan and heat.

4 Stir in capers and arrange round veal.

Veal gratinée

Cooking time   15 minutes

You will need:

4 veal chops	knob butter
4 slices cheese	seasoning

1 Season chops. Spread on 1 side with half the butter and cook until brown.

2 Turn and grill on other side until just cooked.

3 Put slices of cheese over veal and continue cooking until cheese has melted.

4 Serve with green salad.

Veal Imperial

Cooking time   30 minutes

You will need:

4 veal chops
1 oz. butter
seasoning

1 can cream of mushroom
    soup
¼ pint milk
little sherry or lemon juice

1 Brown the veal lightly in the butter.
2 Add soup, milk and seasoning.
3 Cover pan and simmer gently for 25 minutes, adding little extra milk if required.
4 Stir in sherry or lemon juice and serve with rice or creamed potatoes and green salad.

To serve frozen steakburgers

Bean burgers. Fry or grill and top with baked beans.

Cheeseburgers. Fry or grill until nearly ready, then top with slices of cheese and brown until cheese melts.

Kebabs. Divide each steakburger into 4. Put on skewer with bacon rolls and grill.

Steakburgers Mornay. Grill steakburgers. Put on to bed of creamed frozen spinach. Coat with cheese sause (see page 21) and brown under grill.

Steakburgers and tomato. Grill steakburgers on one side. Turn and cover with sliced tomatoes and grill on second side.

To serve canned stewed steak

Canned stewed steak is generally high quality meat and provides a quick meal within minutes. By varying the way it is presented you can avoid monotony.

Steak au gratin   Cooking time 15 minutes

1 Put steak into pan and heat steadily for about 10 minutes.
2 Tip into pie dish.
3 Cover top with biscuit or breadcrumbs and grated or thinly sliced cheese.
4 Brown under grill for 5 minutes.
5 If preferred meat and topping can be heated together in oven for approximately 30 minutes.

Curried steak   Cooking time 15–20 minutes

1 Fry a sliced onion in a knob of fat.
2 Add 2–4 teaspoons curry powder and cook for few minutes.
3 Stir the canned steak into onion mixture.
4 Bring to boil and heat gently for 10 minutes.
5 Add 1 tablespoon chutney to sauce and few sultanas.

Hasty goulash   Cooking time 15 minutes

1 Put steak into pan and heat for 10 minutes.
2 Tip small can of tomatoes in with steak, together with 1 tablespoon paprika pepper blended with 1 tablespoon water.
3 Heat for further 5 minutes.

Steak and marrow   Cooking time 15–20 minutes

can stewed steak   •   little butter or margarine   •   small marrow   •   few breadcrumbs   •   seasoning

1 Peel marrow and cut into rings.
2 Steam or boil until just tender.
3 Meanwhile heat steak.
4 Strain marrow rings, put on to heat resistant dish.
5 Top each ring with steak and crumbs.
6 Dot with a little butter or margarine and brown under grill.

Steak and dumplings   Cooking time 20 minutes

1 Heat the canned steak with ⅓ pint water.
2 Make tiny dumplings by adding 1 oz. shredded suet to 2 oz. self-raising flour and a pinch salt. Mix with water to rolling consistency.

3 Roll in tiny balls—drop into the liquid and cook for 15 minutes.

Pilaf of beef
Cooking time 25 minutes

1 can stewing steak ● 2 oz. rice ● seasoning ● 2 tomatoes ● can of frozen mixed vegetables ● ¾ pint water with little yeast or vegetable extract to flavour ● 1 oz. dripping or margarine ● chopped parsley

1 Skin and slice tomatoes.
2 Heat dripping and fry tomatoes in this.
3 Add water, well flavoured with yeast or beef extract.
4 Bring to the boil.
5 Shake in rice and cook steadily, seasoning well.
6 When rice is tender and has absorbed all liquid add steak and drained vegetables.
7 Heat thoroughly.
8 Garnish with chopped parsley.

Curried corned beef
Cooking time 10–20 minutes

You will need:

12 oz. corned beef	1 tablespoon curry powder
chopped dessert apple	few chopped spring onions
1 oz. margarine OR	(use scissors for speed)
1 tablespoon oil	1 tablespoon chutney

If serving cold you will need a little salad dressing, lettuce, sliced tomatoes, etc.

If serving hot then use a small can mulligatawny soup, some diced cooked potatoes or cooked rice.

1 Heat the oil or margarine, add the onions and apple, toss in the oil for a few minutes; there is no need to cook them until soft.
2 Work in the curry powder and cook for several minutes, then add the chutney and flaked corned beef.

To serve cold:
1 Stir in enough mayonnaise to make a moist consistency.
2 Put on a bed of crisp lettuce (covered with lettuce until the family come home), garnish with sliced tomatoes, radishes, etc.
3 Serve with crisp rolls.

To serve hot:
1 Add the can of soup, potatoes or rice. Make sure you have enough soup to give a moist consistency.
2 Either put the heat very low under the pan, or transfer to a casserole and keep hot in a very slow oven.
3 Put a dish of chutney on the table, some rolls in the oven, so they too are piping hot, and make a big bowl of crisp lettuce salad to serve with this quick curry.
4 If you wish, flaked fish could be used instead of corned beef, hard-boiled eggs (keep these whole), or chopped cooked meat.

Corned beef cutlets
Cooking time 15–20 minutes

You will need:

12 oz. can corned beef	fat for frying
good 2 oz. breadcrumbs	1 oz. margarine
seasoning	1 oz. flour
1 egg	¼ pint milk or stock
crisp breadcrumbs	

1 Make the sauce by heating the margarine in the pan, stirring in the flour and cooking for 2 minutes, then adding the liquid.
2 Bring to the boil and cook until thick.
3 Add the breadcrumbs and the flaked corned beef.
4 Season well.
5 Form into cutlet shapes. Coat with beaten egg and crisp breadcrumbs and fry in hot fat until crisp and golden brown.
6 Serve with fried tomatoes, peas and sauté potatoes.
7 Garnish with cutlet frills.

Lattice beef pie
Cooking time 25 minutes

You will need:

1 can corned beef or left-over beef	3 or 4 spring onions
for cheese sauce	
1 oz. butter	1 oz. flour
seasoning	1 gill milk
4 oz. grated cheese	12 oz.–1 lb. mashed
little extra grated cheese	potato

1 Make thick cheese sauce.
2 Add seasoning, the chopped meat or flaked corned beef and the chopped spring onion. Use some of the green stems too.
3 Put into shallow dish and pipe the potato in a lattice design.
4 Sprinkle the grated cheese over the potato and brown for about 10–15 minutes in a hot oven (425°F.—Gas Mark 6).

Corned beef hash

Cooking time   10–15 minutes

You will need:

12 oz. can corned beef	1 oz. dripping for frying
approximately 8 oz.	sliced beetroot
mashed potatoes	parsley
1 egg	seasoning

1 Flake the corned beef and mix with the potatoes and beaten egg.
2 Season well.
3 Heat the dripping in a pan and put in the mixture.
4 Spread this evenly and allow to cook slowly until the underside is golden brown and the mixture really hot.
5 Fold like an omelette and turn on to a hot dish.
6 Serve garnished with beetroot and parsley.

Ham casserole

As in casserole of steak (see page 26) but use thick slices of cooked ham instead of steak and cook for 5 minutes only before adding bread.
A little sherry is delicious in this recipe.

Ham and potato cakes

Cooking time   15 minutes

You will need:

1 lb. mashed potatoes	few tomatoes
4 slices Gruyère cheese	chopped parsley
seasoning	fat
4 slices ham	

1 Add seasoning and little chopped parsley to the mashed potatoes. If the mixture is dry, then add a little milk and margarine to moisten.
2 Form into 4 large flat cakes, put a little fat on each and brown in a moderately hot oven (400 °F. – Gas Mark 5).
3 Top with a slice of ham and cheese and return to the oven until the cheese is beginning to melt.
4 Decorate with parsley and serve with baked tomatoes.

Cheese and ham pudding

Cooking time   35 minutes

You will need:

2 oz. breadcrumbs	2–3 oz. grated cheese
3–4 oz. chopped ham	3 eggs
clove garlic or slice	1 oz. butter
onion	seasoning
¾ pint milk	

to garnish

sliced cooked tomatoes	chopped parsley

1 Rub saucepan with cut clove of garlic or onion.

2 Put the milk into a saucepan, heat with the crumbs and butter, add cheese, ham, seasoning.
3 Add beaten eggs.
4 Pour into baking dish and cook for approximately 35 minutes in centre of moderate oven (375 °F. – Gas Mark 4) until golden brown and firm.
5 Quickly arrange garnish on top as this pudding is inclined to sink slightly.
6 Serve with crisp toast or creamed potatoes and a green vegetable.

Spiced ham and macédoine of vegetables

Cooking time   15 minutes

You will need:

8 oz. cooked ham	1 packet frozen vegetables
1 oz. butter	2 tablespoons red currant
1 oz. brown sugar	or cranberry jelly
3 tablespoons vinegar	2 teaspoons made
potato crisps	mustard
watercress	good shake pepper

1 Put the butter, vinegar, jelly, sugar and mustard into a saucepan.
2 Heat gently until jelly has melted.
3 Put in the ham and heat through.
4 Meanwhile, cook the mixed vegetables.
5 Serve the ham in its sauce with the vegetables, potato crisps and watercress.

Ham omelette

Cooking time   5 minutes

You will need for 1 person only:

2 eggs	1 oz. ham*
seasoning	good knob of butter

* Cheaper quality ham can be used in this or it is a good way to use up canned luncheon meat.

1 Chop the ham or luncheon meat and mix with the beaten eggs.
2 Heat the knob of butter and pour in the egg mixture.
3 Allow about ½ minute for it to 'set' in a skin at the bottom, then tilt the pan and push the egg liquid backwards and forwards so it drops to the bottom of the pan. Continue until set.
4 Fold or roll away from handle and tip on to hot dish.

Ham in Madeira sauce

Cooking time   10–15 minutes

You will need:

8 thin slices or 4 thick	1 oz. butter
slices of cooked ham	1 LEVEL tablespoon flour

juice 1 orange and
  1 lemon
$\frac{1}{2}$ gill water
	1 gill Madeira
	good pinch, salt, pepper
	  sugar

1 Heat ham under hot grill for a few minutes.
2 Make sauce blending flour with water, then put all other ingredients into pan and cook, stirring well until thick and clear.
3 Pour over ham and serve with heated canned vegetables.

Ham and egg casserole

Cooking time   15 minutes

You will need:

4 hard-boiled eggs
$\frac{1}{2}$ pint white sauce
  (see page 18) (or a can
  of cream of chicken or
  tomato soup)
lettuce
4 tomatoes
	4 oz. cooked chopped
	  ham (or luncheon meat
	  or boiled bacon)
	seasoning
	4 slices toast
	little grated cheese

1 Make white sauce or heat the soup.
2 Add sliced eggs and ham.
3 Season well.
4 Put 4 slices toast in dish. Top with ham mixture, halved tomatoes and cheese.
5 Brown under grill or in the oven.
6 Serve with lettuce.

Devilled ham fritters

Cooking time   20 minutes

You will need:

1 small can chopped ham
  or use about 4 oz.
  fresh ham
4 oz. flour
1 teaspoon curry powder
1 tablespoon chutney
seasoning
	1 gill milk
	2 eggs
	2 or 3 spring onions or
	  chives
	1 teaspoon Worcestershire
	  sauce
	frying fat

1 Sieve flour and curry powder into basin.
2 Add eggs, milk, Worcestershire sauce, chutney

and finely chopped spring onions (use some of the green stems) and ham.
3 Season well.
4 Heat little fat in the pan.
5 Pour in enough mixture to cover pan.
6 Fry steadily until golden brown.
7 Turn and cook on the other side.
8 Pile fritters on a hot dish and serve with salad and tomatoes.

Kidney and macaroni

Cooking time   15–20 minutes

You will need:

4 oz. quick-cooking macaroni 2 oz. grated cheese	parsley to garnish 1 can kidney soup 4 eggs

1 Cook the macaroni for 7 minutes in boiling salted water.
2 Strain and heat with the soup.
3 Put into a shallow casserole.
4 Fry or poach the eggs, arrange on the kidney mixture.
5 Top with grated cheese and brown under the grill.
6 Garnish with parsley.

Tongue in Burgundy sauce

Cooking time   10 minutes

You will need:

4 thick slices cooked tongue 1 gill water seasoning	1 oz. butter 1 oz. flour 1 gill Burgundy

1 Heat butter, stir in flour.
2 Cook for several minutes then gradually add Burgundy, water and seasoning.
3 Bring to boil and cook until thickened.
4 Cut slices of tongue into halves, heat in sauce.
5 Serve with mixed vegetables.

Sauces to serve with meat

Brown sauce Cooking time 10 minutes

Coating Consistency

1 oz. cooking fat or dripping salt and pepper	$\frac{1}{2}$ pint brown stock 1 oz. flour

Panada sauce. As above but use $\frac{1}{4}$ pint brown stock.
Thin sauce. As above but use 1 pint brown stock.

    1 Heat the fat or dripping in a pan. For a better flavour fry a little chopped onion, celery, carrot, in which case use 2 oz. fat.
    2 Add the flour and cook steadily in the fat until brown in colour. Be careful not to overbrown this.
    3 Add stock, carefully stirring all the time, bring to the boil, season and cook until thick and smooth. If vegetables have been used, strain.

Caper sauce Cooking time 5–8 minutes.   As above, but use $\frac{1}{4}$ pint milk and $\frac{1}{4}$ pint stock.
            Add 2 teaspoons capers and little caper vinegar.

Curry sauce Cooking time 30 minutes–1 hour

1 medium-sized onion	1 teaspoon curry paste	1 level tablespoon curry
1 cooking apple	1–2 tablespoons milk or	powder
1 oz. butter	cream*	1 tablespoon desiccated
1 dessertspoon chutney	$\frac{1}{2}$ pint stock or water	coconut
1 level tablespoon	salt	1 dessertspoon sultanas
cornflour		1 teaspoon lemon juice

* This can be omitted with meat curries

1 Chop the onion and cooking apple and sauté in the butter.
2 Add curry powder, paste and cornflour.
3 Stir until blended, cook a few minutes and then stir in stock.
4 Bring to the boil, stirring all the time.
5 Add chutney, coconut and sultanas.
6 Cover and simmer for at least 1 hour.
7 Stir in the lemon juice, add seasoning and the milk or cream.

Horseradish sauce No cooking. Beat bottled horseradish relish or horseradish cream into little cream from top of milk, add few drops lemon juice or vinegar and seasoning.

Tomato sauce Cooking time 10 minutes

		1 small onion
1 small tube or can	2 level teaspoons	$\frac{1}{2}$ pint water
tomato purée	cornflour	good pinch sugar
1 oz. butter or margarine	1 small apple	salt and pepper

1 Heat the butter and fry the chopped onion for a few minutes then the grated, peeled apple.
2 Add the purée, the cornflour blended with the water, and seasoning.
3 Bring to the boil, and stir until smooth.
4 Simmer gently for about 10 minutes, taste and re-season, adding sugar if wished.

Chapter 5   # Savoury Dishes

In this chapter you will find a variety of savoury dishes suitable for light lunch or supper. Although quick and easy to make they contain the essential foods for a well balanced meal and will give you endless variety.

Egg dishes

A quick meal is provided by some form of egg, whether by boiling, frying, poaching, scrambling, or in more elaborate dishes.

Get into the habit of topping creamed potatoes with a chopped hard-boiled egg.

Add a beaten egg to a thickened white or cheese sauce, taking care it does not boil after the egg is added. Just simmer gently for 2 or 3 minutes.

An egg beaten into a glass of hot or cold milk gives one of the quickest and most easily digested meals.

Six new ways to serve scrambled eggs

Cooking time 5–15 minutes

Most people like scrambled eggs, so here are some easy ways of turning them into dishes for supper or breakfast. All are sufficient for 4 people.

Scrambled Eggs de Luxe. To 4 or 5 eggs add 4 tablespoons cream. Season well and cook gently in hot butter.

Scotch Woodcock. Scramble 4 or 5 eggs in the usual way. Serve on hot toast and put anchovy fillets on top.

Mock Crab. Add 2 oz. grated cheese and 1 teaspoon tomato ketchup to 4 beaten eggs. cook lightly. This is delicious as a sandwich filling.

With Vegetables. Heat 1 teacup diced cooked vegetables in hot butter or margarine. Add 4 or 5 well-seasoned and beaten eggs. Cook until just set, pile on toast or creamed potatoes. Sprinkle with grated cheese if wished.

Crisp Scrambled Eggs. Cut 1 or 2 thin slices of bread, remove crusts and cut into tiny dice. Fry in hot butter until golden brown and crisp. Add 4 beaten eggs and cook in usual way— the tiny pieces stay crisp. Add little grated cheese if wished.

With Chicken Liver. Take liver from chicken giblets, chop finely and fry lightly in hot butter or margarine. Add 4 or 5 seasoned eggs and cook in the usual way.
(More scrambled eggs recipes on page 57.)

Baked eggs

Cooking time   5 minutes

1 Butter small oven-proof dishes and break an egg into each.
2 Sprinkle with salt and pepper and grate about $\frac{1}{2}$ oz. cheese on the top.
3 Cover with breadcrumbs and add a small knob of butter.
4 Bake in moderate oven (375°F.—Gas Mark 4) for about 5 minutes.
5 Serve hot.

Buckingham eggs

Cooking time   10 minutes
You will need:

4 slices of bread	little butter for toast
4 eggs	small jar of anchovy paste
2 heaped tablespoons grated cheese	1 oz. margarine or butter
2 tablespoons milk	seasoning

1 Heat knob of butter or margarine in pan.
2 Meanwhile toast the bread, butter and spread it with the paste.
3 Add beaten eggs, milk and seasoning to hot margarine.
4 Scramble lightly, spread on toast and top with the grated cheese.
5 Heat under the grill for a few minutes until the cheese is golden.
6 Serve garnished with watercress.

Cheddar Scotch eggs

Cooking time   15 minutes
You will need:

4 hard-boiled eggs	3 oz. grated Cheddar cheese
little chopped chives or spring onions	tiny knob of butter
little flour	seasoning
1 egg	12 oz. sausage meat
fat for frying	breadcrumbs for coating

1 Shell eggs. Cut into halves very carefully.
2 Remove yolk, put into basin, mash, and add cheese, butter, chives, seasoning.
3 Mix well and press back into white cases.
4 Press the 2 halves together.
5 Divide sausage meat into 4 portions.
6 Flatten on lightly floured board.
7 Put egg on to this then wrap round in sausage meat.
8 Seal 'joints' very firmly.
9 Coat with beaten egg, roll in crumbs.
10 Fry *steadily* in deep fat until golden brown.
11 Drain very well on kitchen paper.

Egg and vegetable cutlets

Cooking time   20 minutes
You will need:

4 or 5 hard-boiled eggs	egg to coat
$\frac{1}{4}$ pint thick white sauce (see page 21)	1 lb. diced and cooked mixed vegetables
breadcrumbs	seasoning

1 Chop eggs, mix with other ingredients and form in 4 or 8 small cutlet shapes.
2 Brush with beaten egg, roll in crisp breadcrumbs and fry until golden brown.
3 Serve hot or cold with salad or cooked vegetables.

Eggs in baked potatoes

1 Scrub and bake large potatoes, 1 for each person.
2 When cooked, take off a slice and scoop out the greater part of the inside, mash this and press back into case making a neat shape.
3 Break eggs carefully, allowing 1 per person.
4 Put an egg into each case.
5 Top with grated cheese and seasoning.
6 Sprinkle with breadcrumbs and add a few tiny pieces of butter.
7 Place in a hot oven until cheese is brown and the eggs set. This takes approximately 15 minutes.

Eggs royale

Cooking time   25 minutes

You will need:

5 hard-boiled eggs
1 onion
4 oz. grated cheese
little milk
olives
small packet frozen beans

1 can condensed chicken
    soup
2 oz. butter
1 green pepper (or use
    cooked peas)

1 Heat the soup with just a little milk, add the beans, which should be lightly cooked.
2 Slice and fry the onion in the butter, then add the chopped pepper or cooked peas.
3 When tender, stir into the soup mixture together with 4 of the chopped hard-boiled eggs.
4 Arrange in a casserole and serve garnished with the last egg and sliced olives.

MAKING AN OMELETTE

Cooking time   5–8 minutes

Allow 1½–2 eggs per person

1 Beat eggs in a basin. Break each separately in a cup before transferring to basin (in case any are bad).
2 Add a good pinch salt and pepper, and for each 1½–2 eggs 1 tablespoon of water.
3 Put knob of butter into omelette pan and when hot pour in eggs. Leave for about 1 minute over high heat to allow bottom to set, then loosen egg mixture from sides of pan and cook rapidly, tipping pan from side to side so that the liquid egg flows underneath and cooks quickly.
4 When egg is set as you like it (tastes vary) slip palette knife under omelette and fold it away from handle of pan.
5 Grasp handle firmly and tip on to a hot plate.

Cheese omelette. Add grated cheese just before folding the omelette or use soft cream cheese.

Fish omelette. Heat flaked cooked fish or shell fish with a little butter and cream from top of milk. Add to omelette just before folding.

Meat omelette. Chop cooked meat very finely and add to beaten eggs, together with a little mustard as well as salt and pepper.

Mushroom omelette. Fry chopped mushrooms in a little butter. Add to beaten eggs.

Vegetable omelette. Either add chopped cooked vegetables to beaten eggs before cooking or heat the vegetables with a little butter, white or cheese sauce and add to omelette before folding.

Spanish omelette and fried rice

Cooking time   25 minutes

You will need:

6 eggs
chopped parsley
4 oz. rice
2 oz. butter
little olive oil
extra butter
seasoning

small can mixed vegetables
small can tuna fish,
    prawns or shrimps, or
    use several rashers of
    bacon
1 small finely chopped
    onion

1 First put on the rice to cook in boiling salted water, strain when just tender.
2 Heat a little butter and oil together and fry the rice until golden.
3 Heat the butter in the omelette pan, fry the onion and chopped bacon.
4 Add the flaked fish and drained vegetables to the egg and pour into the pan.
5 Cook steadily on the underside and when this seems firm put under a warmed grill to set the top side.
6 Serve with the rice.

Piquante eggs

Cooking time   25 minutes

You will need:

4 hard-boiled eggs
½ pint white sauce
    (see page 21)
2 tablespoons bread-
    crumbs
1 oz. margarine

2 tablespoons tomato
    ketchup
2 thinly sliced onions
2 tablespoons grated
    cheese

1 Heat the margarine and fry the sliced onions until just soft.
2 Put at the bottom of a dish with the shelled and halved hard-boiled eggs on top.
3 Mix the tomato ketchup into the hot, but not boiling, white sauce.
4 Season well and pour over the eggs.
5 Top with grated cheese and breadcrumbs and brown in the oven or under the grill.
6 If wished a little chopped cooked bacon can be mixed with the onions.

POACHED AND FRIED EGGS

Method of poaching eggs and other suggestions, see page 57.

Tomato poached eggs Cooking time 8 minutes

1 Heat a can of tomato soup in a shallow pan adding little water if too thick.
2 Break 3 or 4 eggs into this and poach in usual way.
3 Serve with toast.

Curried poached eggs

1 Heat a can mulligatawny soup in a shallow pan, adding little water if too thick.
2 Break 3 or 4 eggs into this and cook in usual way.
3 Serve with rice.

Cheese topped fried egg

1 Fry eggs in usual way, but just before setting put slices of cheese into pan.
2 Serve eggs on toast topped with cheese.

Fried egg fingers

1 Beat eggs, season well and pour into shallow dish.
2 Cut fingers of bread and remove crusts.
3 Soak in the egg until this is quite absorbed. Lift egg fingers carefully into hot fat and fry. This often appeals to people who do not like ordinary fried eggs.

Surprise eggs

Cooking time	10 minutes

You will need:

6 eggs	12 rounds bread and butter

filling

seasoning	4 oz. cooked ham
2 oz. finely chopped cooked mushrooms	(minced or chopped) tomato to garnish

1 Hard-boil and halve the eggs.
2 Cut small thin slices off the bottom to make them stand and remove the yolks.
3 Make a purée of the ham, mix with egg yolks, and chopped mushrooms and season.
4 Fill egg cases with mixture.
5 Garnish with tomato.
6 Serve with brown bread and butter.

Swiss eggs

Cooking time	12–15 minutes

You will need:

4 or 5 oz. processed Gruyère cheese	little butter triangles of fried bread
2 or 3 tablespoons cream	4 eggs seasoning

1 Butter a shallow dish and line it with sliced Gruyère cheese.
2 Break the eggs carefully and slide on top of the cheese.
3 Cover with cream, seasoning and the rest of the Gruyère cheese, which should be grated or finely chopped.

4 Bake in a moderately hot oven (400 °F. – Gas Mark 5) for about 12 minutes until the eggs are set.
5 Serve at once, garnished with triangles of crisply fried bread.

WAYS TO SERVE CHEESE

Whether cheese is served uncooked or in a variety of cooked dishes it is a first class protein food.

Many people who find pieces of cheese indigestible will eat it more readily if grated. This is particularly suitable when serving cheese in salads.

Take care that cheese is NOT overcooked; when adding to a sauce it should be heated gently, not boiled.

Serve a variety of cheese, so it does not become dull and monotonous.

Cheese and carrot fingers

Cooking time	10 minutes

You will need:

4 slices of bread	2 good-sized grated
butter	carrots
seasoning	chopped parsley
4–6 oz. grated cheese	

1 Mix the grated carrot and most of the cheese together with enough butter to bind.
2 Season well. Toast the bread.
3 Spread on top of crisp toast.
4 Cover with the rest of the cheese and brown.
5 Garnish with chopped parsley.

Cheese Charlotte

Cooking time	30 minutes

You will need:

6–8 oz. grated cheese —use all Cheddar or $\frac{2}{3}$ Cheddar and $\frac{1}{3}$ Parmesan cheese	3 large thin slices bread and butter 1 egg $\frac{1}{2}$ pint milk
seasoning tomato	parsley

1 Cut triangles from the bread and butter.
2 Arrange half of these at bottom of pie dish.
3 Sprinkle with half the cheese.
4 Arrange remainder of bread and butter on top of this, cover with rest of cheese.
5 Beat egg, add milk and season well.
6 Pour over bread and cheese mixture.
7 Bake for about 30 minutes in moderate oven.

Cheese croquettes

Cooking time   30 minutes

You will need:

6–8 oz. grated cheese	1 teaspoon chopped
3–4 oz. breadcrumbs	parsley
1 egg	thick white sauce (made
seasoning	from 1 oz. margarine,
fat for frying	1 oz. flour, ¼ pint milk)
1 teaspoon grated onion	

1 Add cheese, onion, parsley and half crumbs to the warm white sauce, together with the egg yolk.
2 When mixture is cool, form into 8 finger shapes.
3 Brush with egg white and roll in the rest of the crumbs.
4 Fry until crisp and golden brown.
5 Serve hot or cold.

Cheese and egg meringues

1 Toast slices of bread on 1 side only.
2 Place untoasted side uppermost, and butter.
3 Separate yolks from whites.
4 Beat whites until stiff and form into a ring on the bread.
5 Drop the yolk into the centre.
6 Season and cover with grated cheese.
7 Place in a moderately hot oven (400 °F. – Gas Mark 5) for about 10 minutes until set.

Cheese and egg ring

Cooking time   20 minutes

You will need:

4 eggs	8 oz. grated Cheddar
1 oz. butter	cheese
1 oz. flour	8 oz. sliced cooked green
scant ½ pint milk	beans (fresh or frozen)
	4–6 oz. rice

1 Put rice into boiling salted water and cook for 15–20 minutes (until tender).
2 Meanwhile hard-boil the eggs.
3 Shell the eggs.
4 Cut into 8 lengthwise.
5 Melt the butter in small saucepan.
6 Stir in the flour and cook gently for 1 minute.
7 Add the milk a little at a time, stirring constantly until the sauce is creamy and has thickened.
8 Remove from heat, add 6 oz. grated cheese, half the sliced green beans and the hard-boiled eggs.
9 Stir gently until the eggs have heated through.
10 Pour into a ring of well drained rice.
11 Arrange rest of beans round rice.
12 Sprinkle with remaining cheese.
13 Serve at once.

Cheese frankfurters

Cooking time   10 minutes

You will need:

8 frankfurters	8 oz. cheese
8 slices bacon	

1 Cut a lengthwise slit in each frankfurter.
2 Cut strip of cheese the length of frankfurter and about ¼ inch thick.
3 Fill slit with strip of cheese, wrap slice of bacon around each frankfurter and fasten ends with toothpicks.
4 Grill frankfurters slowly, turning often, until the bacon and frankfurters are cooked through and browned.

Cheese and marrow savoury

Cooking time   20 minutes

You will need:

1 or 2 young marrows	8 oz. grated cheese
1 oz. butter	1 level tablespoon flour
4 tomatoes	½ gill water
seasoning	

1 Slice marrow into rings.
2 Take out seeds but do not remove peel if very young.
3 Sprinkle with salt.
4 Steam over boiling water until tender.
5 Meanwhile, fry sliced tomatoes in butter.
6 Blend flour with water, add to tomato mixture and cook until thick, but smooth.
7 Stir in 6 oz. cheese and seasoning.
8 Arrange marrow rings on dish, cover with cheese mixture.
9 Sprinkle with grated cheese and brown under grill or in oven.
10 Serve with young vegetables.

Cream cheese mould

No cooking – just dissolving gelatine

You will need:

¼ pint tomato juice or	½ gill water
evaporated milk or	4 oz. finely grated cheese
milk according to	or cream cheese
taste	seasoning
1 teaspoon chopped	2 tablespoons powder
parsley	gelatine
1 teaspoon chopped	
gherkins	

1 Beat tomato juice or milk very gradually into cheese until smooth mixture.
2 Dissolve the gelatine in the *hot* water.
3 Add to cheese with seasoning, parsley and gherkins.
4 Pour into tiny moulds and when set, turn out and serve with salad.

Cheese and onion fritters

Cooking time   10 minutes

You will need:

4 eggs	1 oz. dripping or
4 oz. grated cheese	vegetable shortening
seasoning	½ gill tomato ketchup
¼ pint white sauce	2 oz. dripping or
(see page 21)	vegetable shortening
1 grated onion	for frying
2 oz. flour	

1 Fry onion until soft in 1 oz. dripping.
2 Add to beaten eggs with flour, grated cheese, seasoning.
3 Beat until smooth.
4 Heat some of the shortening in frying pan.
5 Drop in 3 separate spoonfuls of mixture and cook until golden on underside, turn and cook on other side.
6 Drain and put on hot dish.
7 Continue cooking like this until all mixture is used.
8 Meanwhile make white sauce, add ketchup and heat without boiling.
9 Arrange on flat dish, serve sauce separately.

Cheese pilaff

Cooking time   25 minutes

You will need:

4–6 oz. Patna rice	6 oz. mushrooms
3 large tomatoes	6–8 oz. grated or diced
2 large onions	cheese
seasoning	1–1½ pints water
3 oz. butter	

1 Heat half the butter in pan.
2 Fry sliced onions until nearly soft.
3 Add skinned sliced tomatoes.
4 Cook for several minutes, then add water.
5 Bring to the boil, shake in the rice, season well and cook until tender (approximately 15–20 minutes), stir well as mixture thickens.
6 Meanwhile, fry mushrooms in rest of the butter.
7 Stir cheese into rice mixture.
8 Pile on to hot dish surrounded with mushrooms.

Cheese and potato soufflé

Cooking time   30 minutes

You will need:

12 oz. mashed potato	seasoning
2 eggs	2 tablespoons milk
1 oz. margarine or butter	1 teaspoon finely chopped
3–4 oz. grated cheese	chives or grated onion

1 Mash the potatoes well.
2 Add the margarine, cheese, milk and chives, then season well.
3 Stir in the well-beaten egg yolks and, when the mixture is cool, *fold* in stiffly beaten egg white.

4 Put into a well-greased soufflé dish, bake in the centre of a moderately hot oven (400 °F. – Gas Mark 5) for 30 minutes until well risen and crisp and brown on top.

Cheese rissoles

Cooking time   10–15 minutes

You will need:

1 oz. butter	6 oz. grated cheese
1 oz. flour	2 teaspoons chopped
¼ pint milk	parsley
seasoning	pinch mixed herbs
1 egg	2 oz. soft breadcrumbs
fat for frying	crisp breadcrumbs

1 Heat butter in pan, stir in flour and cook for several minutes.
2 Gradually add milk, bring to boil, cook until thick.
3 Season well, add crumbs, cheese, parsley, herbs.
4 Cool mixture, form either into rounds or finger shapes, coat in beaten egg and crumbs.
5 Fry in hot fat until crisp and brown.

Cheese scones

Cooking time   10 minutes

You will need:

6 oz. flour (with plain	pinch mustard
flour add 2 teaspoons	2–3 oz. grated cheese
baking powder)	seasoning
1 oz. margarine or butter	milk to mix
or cooking fat	

1 Sieve flour, baking powder and good pinch of salt, pepper, mustard.
2 Rub in margarine, add cheese and enough milk to make a soft, rolling consistency.
3 Roll out to about ½–¾ inch thick.
4 Cut into desired shapes and bake on lightly greased tins for about 10 minutes in a very hot oven (475°F.—Gas Mark 8).
5 When cool, split and butter.

Cheese rusks

Cooking time   14 minutes

1 Make as for cheese scones, but rather thinner, about ¼ inch thick.
2 Cook for a good 5–7 minutes until brown on outside in moderately hot oven (425°F.—Gas Mark 6).
3 Remove from trays and split carefully through middle.
4 Put CUT side downwards on the tray and cook for a further 5–7 minutes.

Cheese and salmon mould

Cooking time   1 hour

You will need:

2 oz. breadcrumbs
1 gill milk
1 medium can salmon
seasoning
little chopped parsley

2 oz. grated cheese
1 egg
1 small onion
1 oz. margarine

1 Fry the finely chopped onion in the margarine.
2 Flake the fish and mix with all other ingredients.
3 Put into well greased loaf tin.
4 Cover with greased paper and bake for approximately 45 minutes in centre of moderate oven (375°F.—Gas Mark 5).
5 Turn out and serve with baked tomatoes, peas and creamed potatoes.

Cheese and shrimp fritters

Cooking time   5 minutes

You will need:

4 oz. shrimps
(frozen or canned)

6 oz. grated Cheddar
cheese
fat for frying

fritter batter

4 oz. plain flour
¼ pint milk

salt and pepper
1 egg

1 Sieve flour and seasonings into a basin.
2 Gradually beat in milk and lightly beaten egg.
3 Stir in the cheese and shrimps.
4 Place in teaspoon in the hot fat.
5 Fry until crisp and golden brown.
6 Drain well and serve at once.

Cold cheese soufflé

Cooking time   10 minutes

You will need:

2 egg yolks
3 egg whites
¼ pint milk
salt and pepper
mustard
1½ dessertspoons
   powder gelatine
gherkins

6–8 oz. finely grated
   Cheshire or Cheddar
   cheese
¼ pint cream or
   evaporated milk
½ gill water or white
   stock
tomatoes

1 Beat egg yolks.
2 Add milk and cook gently until mixture coats back of spoon, add cheese while still hot.
3 Dissolve gelatine in very hot water or stock.
4 Add to cheese mixture.
5 Cool then fold in lightly whipped cream or evaporated milk, seasoning and lastly the stiffly beaten egg whites.
6 Pour into prepared buttered soufflé dish.
7 Leave until set.

8 Garnish with flower shapes in gherkin and tomato, serve with salad and thin bread and butter.

Cream cheese and prawn soufflé

You will need:

ingredients as in preceding recipe
but use
6 oz. cream cheese

½ pint chopped prawns
watercress

1 Blend cream cheese with milk until smooth.
2 Pour on to the egg yolks, continue as before.
3 Add the prawns before the cream.
4 Pour into 4 small dishes and when set garnish with prawns and tiny springs of watercress.

Cheese and spinach soufflé

Cooking time   35 minutes

You will need:

¼ pint thick white
   sauce (see page 21)
4 oz. grated cheese
seasoning
1 teaspoon oil
3 eggs

¼ pint cooked and
   chopped spinach (frozen
   spinach is ideal)
1 teaspoon finely chopped
   onion or chopped chives

1 Heat the oil and fry the onion in this then mix with the sauce, spinach, grated cheese, seasoning and the beaten egg yolks.
2 FOLD in the stiffly beaten egg whites.
3 Pour into a greased soufflé dish and bake in the middle of a moderate oven (375 °F. – Gas Mark 4) for 35 minutes.

Cheese and tomato ring

No cooking

You will need:

packet aspic jelly
¼ pint evaporated milk
salt
4 large tomatoes
¼ pint water
garnish
radishes
lettuce

½ pint milk
8 oz. cream or grated
   cheese
pepper
mustard

tomatoes

1 Dissolve the aspic jelly in the boiling water.
2 Cool slightly then whisk in milk, cheese and lastly, when cool, the lightly whipped evaporated milk.
3 Taste and season.
4 When the mixture is just beginning to thicken add chopped tomato pulp.
5 Put into ring mould.
6 When set turn out and garnish with water-lilies of radish and tomato and lettuce.

Cheese and vegetable cutlets

Cooking time   25 minutes

You will need:

1 oz. margarine or butter	egg or milk for coating
1 oz. flour	the cutlets
$\frac{1}{4}$ pint milk	approximately
4 oz. grated cheese	2 tablespoons soft
about 8 oz. cooked	breadcrumbs
mixed vegetables—	crisp breadcrumbs for
as many as possible	coating
oil for frying if desired	

1 Heat the margarine in a saucepan, stir in the flour and cook for several minutes.
2 Take the pan off the heat and gradually add the cold milk.
3 Return to the heat and bring slowly to the boil, stirring all the time to keep the sauce smooth.
4 Add the seasoning and the vegetables which should be diced.
5 Next, add the grated cheese and enough of the soft breadcrumbs to make a mixture that is firm enough to handle without being too dry.
6 When cold, mould into about 6 cutlet shapes, brush with milk or a little beaten egg and coat in crisp breadcrumbs.
7 Heat the oil in a frying pan and fry the cutlets until crisp and brown.
8 Serve with green peas and creamed potatoes.
9 If preferred, the cutlets can be put on to a hot greased baking tin and crisped in a hot oven (450°F.—Gas Mark 7) for about 10–15 minutes.

Cheeseolettes

Cooking time   10 minutes

You will need:

3 eggs	4 oz. grated cheese
2 oz. flour (with plain	1 tablespoon grated onion
flour use $\frac{1}{2}$ teaspoon	2 tablespoons chopped
baking powder)	parsley
fat, oil or shortening	seasoning
for frying	

1 Blend all the ingredients together.
2 Heat fat in pan and drop in spoonfuls of this mixture.
3 Fry until crisp and golden brown.
4 Turn, brown on the other side.
5 Drain well and serve with a dish of sliced tomatoes and another of crisp lettuce.
These are a cross between pancakes and omelettes.

English monkey

Cooking time   10 minutes

You will need:

4 slices toast	4 oz. grated cheese
1 oz. butter	2 eggs
$\frac{1}{2}$ gill milk	mustard
2 oz. soft breadcrumbs	Worcestershire sauce
2 tablespoons cream	1 tomato

1 Heat butter in a pan.
2 Add milk and breadcrumbs.
3 When very hot add the grated cheese and beaten egg.
4 Season well, adding a little made mustard and few drops Worcestershire sauce.
5 Stir together until thick and creamy.
6 Pour on to toast, garnish with sliced tomatoes.

Gourmet macaroni cheese

Cooking time   10–15 minutes

You will need for 3–4 servings:

4 oz. quick cooking	salt and pepper to taste
macaroni	$\frac{1}{2}$ can milk (or water)
1 can condensed	6 oz. grated cheese
tomato soup	1 can crab meat (optional)

1 Cook macaroni for 7 minutes in boiling salted water.
2 Drain.
3 Heat soup and milk in saucepan.
4 Add crab meat and macaroni and half the grated cheese.
5 Season to taste.
6 Pour into serving dish.
7 Top with remaining cheese.
8 Brown under grill.

Macaroni ring

Cooking time   10–15 minutes

You will need:

6 oz. quick cooking	3 tomatoes
macaroni	1 finely chopped onion
4 oz. cooked ham	1 oz. butter
seasoning	

for the cheese sauce

1 oz. butter	1 oz. flour
$\frac{1}{2}$ pint milk	6 oz. diced or grated
seasoning	cheese

1 Chop onion or grate it.
2 Put the quick cooking macaroni into boiling salted water and cook for 7 minutes only.
3 Meanwhile make the cheese sauce.
4 Strain the macaroni and melt the butter in the pan, fry the onion, add the sliced tomatoes, then the macaroni and diced ham.
5 Heat together and form into a round.
6 Fill with the cheese sauce and serve at once.

Pebbles on the beach

Cooking time   30 minutes

You will need:

3 hard-boiled eggs	6 cooked new potatoes
½ pint white sauce	2–3 oz. grated Cheshire or
(see page 21)	Cheddar cheese
1–2 oz. butter	chopped parsley
2 oz. breadcrumbs	seasoning

1 Cut eggs and potatoes in halves crosswise and arrange them flat side down, in a fireproof dish.
2 Season sauce well and add grated cheese.
3 Pour the sauce over the eggs and potatoes, heat through in moderately hot oven for about 20 minutes.
4 Decorate with crumbs fried in the butter and parsley.

Quick macaroni fritters

Cooking time   15 minutes

You will need:

2 oz. quick cooking	seasoning
macaroni	little fat for frying
3 eggs	can condensed celery
4 oz. grated cheese	or tomato soup

1 Cook macaroni in boiling salted water for 7 minutes.
2 Drain well.
3 Beat eggs and cheese and seasoning.
4 Mix in macaroni.
5 Heat fat in frying pan and drop in spoonfuls of this mixture.
6 Fry until crisp and golden, turn and brown other side.
7 Drain and serve with salad or can of undiluted soup.

Savoury celery rarebit

Cooking time   10–15 minutes

You will need:

1 medium-sized stick	1 tablespoon of beer
of celery or a can of	or ale OR
celery hearts	1 dessertspoon
1 oz. margarine or butter	Worcestershire sauce
1 gill milk—or celery	4 slices of toast
stock	6 oz. grated cheese
½ oz. flour	seasoning (including
	mustard)

1 Melt margarine in pan, stir in flour and cook until roux is dry.
2 Add cold milk, bring to boil and cook until very thick.
3 Season well, adding sauce or beer and nearly all the cheese.
4 Cut the celery into neat pieces, cook in boiling salted water until just soft or heat thoroughly if canned.

5 Arrange the pieces on the hot slices of toast and put the rarebit mixture on top.
6 Sprinkle with remainder of cheese.
7 Brown under a hot grill.

Vermicelli with cream cheese sauce

Cooking time   15 minutes

You will need:

4–6 oz. vermicelli

for the sauce

3 tablespoons finely	1¼ gills boiling water
chopped parsley	2 oz. butter
3 oz. grated Cheddar	8 oz. soft cream cheese
cheese	1 crushed clove garlic or
seasoning	chopped small onion

1 Cook the vermicelli in boiling salted water until just tender.
2 Meanwhile put all the ingredients for the sauce into a basin, except the boiling water.
3 Mix very thoroughly, then gradually blend in the boiling water and stir until smooth sauce.
4 Dish up the pasta and serve with the sauce and grated cheese.

Asparagus with mousseline sauce

Cooking time   25 minutes

You will need:

1 medium-sized bunch	either 1 large egg or the
of asparagus—cooked	yolks of 2 eggs
and drained	1 dessertspoon lemon
¼ gill cream from the	juice
top of the milk	seasoning
1 oz. margarine or butter	

1 Cook asparagus.
2 Put all the ingredients for sauce into a basin over hot water.
3 Cook until thickened.
4 Serve at once poured over asparagus or in a sauce boat.

Baked soufflé potatoes

Cooking time   1¼ hours

You will need:

4 large potatoes	1 tablespoon cream
2 egg yolks	seasoning
peas	2 stiffly beaten egg whites

1 Wash the potatoes and bake until tender, about one hour.

2 Cut off tops, scoop out pulp and sieve or mash until soft.

3 Add the yolks of egg, cream or top of milk, seasoning and the stiffly beaten egg whites.

4 Pile back into the potato cases and cook for 15 minutes until just pale golden brown.

5 Serve garnished with peas.

Barbecued beans

Cooking time	10 minutes

You will need:

small can tomatoes	2 large cans beans in
2 onions	tomato sauce
4 rashers bacon	little chopped parsley
seasoning	1 oz. butter

1 Chop onions finely and toss in the hot butter until tender.

2 Add diced bacon and cook until crisp, then stir in the can of tomatoes and cook for several minutes.

3 Add beans and heat thoroughly.

4 Keep very hot, adding parsley and seasoning before serving.

Beetroot cups

No cooking

You will need:

4 cooked beetroots	2 tablespoons chopped
2 oz. cooked peas	radishes
2 oz. cooked diced	1 tablespoon chopped
young carrots	spring onions
seasoning	French dressing
sliced cucumber	(see page 63)

1 Scoop out centre of beetroot and dice.

2 Moisten beetroot cases with French dressing.

3 Mix peas, carrots, radishes, onion and diced beetroot.

4 Season well, toss in French dressing and pile mixture in beetroot cases.

5 Put on dish with a border of sliced cucumber.

6 Serve at once so beetroot does not discolour the filling.

Cauliflower savoury

Cooking time	25 minutes

You will need:

1 large cauliflower	seasoning
4 mushrooms	4 large tomatoes
$\frac{1}{2}$ pint white sauce	1 large onion
(see page 21)	2 oz. butter or margarine
4 oz. grated cheese	2 hard-boiled eggs

for sauce

1 oz. butter	1 oz. flour
$\frac{1}{3}$ pint milk	seasoning

1 Divide cauliflower into flowerets.

2 Boil in boiling salted water until only just tender.

3 Fry the sliced onion, tomatoes and chopped mushrooms in butter, season well.

4 Arrange half the cauliflower in hot dish.

5 Cover with mushroom mixture.

6 Arrange rest of flowerets over the top in a round cauliflower shape.

7 Cover with white sauce and cheese.

8 Brown in oven or under grill.

9 Garnish with quartered tomatoes and hard-boiled eggs.

Cauliflower and tomato fritters

Cooking time	20 minutes

You will need:

1 large cauliflower	$\frac{1}{4}$ pint tomato juice or
1 egg	2 tablespoons
seasoning	concentrated tomato
fat for frying	purée diluted with
4 oz. flour (preferably	enough water to make
plain)	$\frac{1}{4}$ pint

1 Sieve flour, add egg, tomato liquid and seasoning.

2 Beat well.

3 Divide the cauliflower into fairly even flowerets.

4 Cook in a little boiling salted water until just tender.

5 Drain well, being careful not to let the flowerets break.

6 Coat each piece of cauliflower with the batter.

7 Lower into hot fat (shallow fat will be very satisfactory) and cook on both sides until crisp and golden brown.

8 Drain well.

Devilled mushroom and egg

Cooking time	15 minutes

You will need:

4 rounds toast	good pinch curry powder
2 oz. mushrooms	$\frac{1}{2}$–1 teaspoon made
3 hard-boiled eggs	mustard
2 oz. butter	1 teaspoon mustard
1 teaspoon Worcester-	ketchup
shire sauce	

1 Heat butter.

2 Fry chopped mushrooms in it, add flavourings.

3 When mushrooms are cooked add quartered hard-boiled eggs.

4 Heat and serve at once on toast.

Noodle and mushroom ring

Cooking time   30 minutes

You will need:

8 oz. noodles	¾ gill milk
2 eggs	2 oz. grated cheese
seasoning	

for the filling

½ pint milk	1 oz. flour
4–6 oz. mushrooms	seasoning
1 oz. margarine or butter	

1 Put the noodles into boiling salted water and cook for 15 minutes.
2 Drain, then mix with well-beaten eggs, milk, seasoning and grated cheese.
3 Put this mixture either into a double saucepan or a basin over hot water and cook gently until eggs have set, stirring well.
4 This will take approximately 15 minutes, for it is important that the mixture does not boil.
5 Form into the shape of a ring.
6 Skin the mushrooms but leave them whole, put into the milk together with a little seasoning and simmer gently until mushrooms are just tender.
7 Take them out of the milk and keep hot.
8 Measure the milk and make it up to ½ pint again.
9 Blend it with the flour, put into the saucepan together with the margarine and seasoning and, stirring all the time, bring to the boil.
10 Cook until the sauce thickens, then replace the mushrooms in the saucepan.
11 Heat in the sauce and pour into the centre of the noodle ring.

Potato basket

Cooking time   45 minutes

You will need:

1½ lb. potatoes	milk
1 lb. cooked vegetables	margarine
(as varied a mixture	1 egg
as possible)	½ pint thick white sauce
4 oz. grated cheese	(see page 21)

1 Beat the potatoes until light and fluffy, adding milk and margarine.
2 Pipe or mould into a square shape with a hollow centre and brush with well-beaten egg.
3 Add the vegetables and cheese to half the sauce and heat thoroughly.
4 Pile this mixture in the centre of the 'basket'.
5 Pour the remainder of the sauce over the top and garnish with 1 large, whole mushroom.

Savoury macaroni or spaghetti

Cooking time   15 minutes

This is an excellent alternative to potatoes when they are scarce.

You will need:

4 oz. quick cooking	2 oz. margarine
macaroni	1 very thinly sliced onion
2 teaspoons chopped	2 teaspoons capers
parsley	

1 Cook macaroni, strain.
2 Meanwhile fry sliced onion in plenty of margarine in pan.
3 Add macaroni, parsley and capers.
4 Serve round meat.

Savoury stuffed onions

Cooking time   1¼ hours

You will need:

4 medium-sized onions	1 or 2 fresh eggs
1 teaspoon sage	3 oz. grated cheese
1½ oz margarine	seasoning
4 oz. breadcrumbs	

1 Put the onions into salted water and boil steadily for 30 minutes. By this time they will not be completely cooked but it should be possible to remove the centre core.
2 Keep stock.
3 Chop the core of the onion finely, add the remaining ingredients and pile this stuffing back into the centre cavity.
4 Put the onions into a greased casserole.
5 Pour over ½ gill of the onion stock and put a small piece of margarine on top of each onion.
6 Bake for 45 minutes in the covered dish at 400°F. – Gas Mark 5.
7 Serve with cheese sauce (see page 21). Garnish with parsley.

Spinach pancakes

Cooking time   15 minutes

You will need:

4 oz. flour	1 oz. butter
1–2 eggs	½ pint white sauce
½ pint milk	(see page 21)
seasoning	3 oz. grated cheese or
fat for frying	4 oz. chopped ham
1 lb. cooked and well-drained spinach	

1 Sieve or chop the spinach and reheat with the butter.

2 Mix the flour, eggs, milk and seasoning together.

3 Pour a little of this batter in hot fat in the pan and cook for several minutes until crisp and brown.

4 Turn or toss and cook on the other side.

5 Fill each pancake with some of the spinach.

6 Keep hot on a dish over a pan of water.

7 When all the pancakes are cooked, add cheese or ham to the white sauce and pour it over the top.

Note: If preferred, all the pancakes may be kept and spread with spinach, then piled on top of each other in which case cut large slices as you would a cake, to serve.

Spinach ring

Cooking time   30 minutes

You will need:

2 lb. spinach	2 oz. soft breadcrumbs
1 egg	1 onion
seasoning	2 oz. butter

1 Cook the spinach with only the water left on the leaves after washing and a little salt.

2 When cooked, drain well and either sieve or chop finely.

3 Meanwhile fry the chopped onion in the hot butter until tender, add the spinach, crumbs and egg.

4 Season well.

5 Form into a ring and set in a hot oven.

6 Fill the centre with 1 of the fillings below and garnish with a ring of chopped hard-boiled egg.

Hard-boiled egg sauce: Stir 3 chopped hard-boiled eggs into ½ pint white sauce, (see page 21). Pour into centre of spinach ring and garnish with sliced and chopped hard-boiled egg.

Cheese filling: Fill ring with ½ pint thick cheese sauce (see page 21). Garnish with tomato or bacon rolls.

Creamed ham: 6 oz. chopped ham heated in ¼ pint white sauce (see page 21).

Creamed chicken: As above, using chicken instead of ham.

Creamed prawns: Use 1 pint prawns instead of ham.

Savoury egg: Fry 2 sliced onions and 2 skinned, sliced tomatoes until soft in a little butter or margarine. Add 3–4 beaten eggs, season and cook until eggs are lightly scrambled.

Stuffed baked beetroot

Cooking time   15 minutes

You will need:

4 medium-sized cooked beetroots	tomato, watercress and hard-boiled egg for garnishing
2 oz. grated cheese	2 oz. butter or margarine
2 oz. breadcrumbs	
seasoning	

1 Cut a slice off the bottom of each beetroot so that they stand well.

2 Scoop out a little from the centre of each one. These pieces can be used in salad.

3 Cream margarine, add seasoning, crumbs and cheese.

4 Press into the centre of the beetroot and stand in a well-greased dish.

5 Bake for 15 minutes in a moderately hot oven (400°F.—Gas Mark 5) until cheese melts slightly.

6 Garnish with watercress, tomato rings and sliced hard-boiled eggs.

Stuffed cauliflower

Cooking time   35 minutes

You will need:

1 medium-sized cauliflower	2 oz. margarine or butter
⅓ pint milk	1 oz. flour
1 small onion sliced very thinly	4 or 5 chopped mushrooms
1 oz. breadcrumbs	3 oz. grated cheese
new potatoes	seasoning
	parsley

1 Cook the cauliflower whole in boiling salted water until just soft. Cut a piece off the bottom if necessary, to make sure it stands firm.

2 Scoop out part of the centre and chop it finely.

3 Heat 1 oz. margarine, add the flour and cook for several minutes, then gradually add the milk.

4 Bring to the boil, cook until thickened, add seasoning and 2 oz. cheese.

5 Fry onion and mushrooms in the remainder of margarine until soft, stir in crumbs, chopped cauliflower and enough sauce to bind.

6 Press in centre of cauliflower.

7 Pour rest of sauce over the top, sprinkle with the rest of the cheese.

8 Put in a moderately hot oven (400°F.—Gas Mark 5) for 15 minutes until golden brown.

9 Serve with new potatoes and garnish with parsley.

Stuffed mushrooms

Cooking time   10 minutes

You will need:

12 large mushrooms	4 slices buttered toast
3 eggs	few capers if desired
little milk	seasoning
1½ oz. butter	little fat for mushrooms

1 Fry the mushrooms in the fat.
2 Chop the stalks and cook in the butter, then add the eggs, beaten with the milk and seasoning.
3 Scramble lightly.
4 Add the capers, then pile into the mushroom caps.
5 Arrange on toast.

Stuffed tomatoes

Cooking time   approximately 15 minutes

There are innumerable ways of using stuffed tomatoes as main dishes. Here are some of the most interesting. Remember to season the tomato case before putting in the filling.

Hot.
Spanish tomatoes. Remove pulp from large tomatoes, mix with diced ham, egg, little brown gravy, lots of seasoning and a little grated onion or crushed garlic. Bake for 10–15 minutes in moderately hot oven.
Indian tomatoes. Mix pulp with cooked rice, little curry powder and onion fried in hot fat. Bake for 10–15 minutes in moderately hot oven.
Provençale tomatoes. Mix pulp with fried onion, grated cheese, breadcrumbs and seasoning. Bake for 10–15 minutes.
Au gratin. Mix pulp with breadcrumbs, seasoning, grated cheese and an egg if wished. Top with breadcrumbs, grated cheese and a little butter or margarine. Bake for 10–15 minutes.

Cold.
With shrimps or prawns. Mix pulp with shrimps or prawns (or cooked white fish) add mayonnaise, seasoning, chopped parsley, also capers and chopped gherkin if wished. Serve with crisp lettuce leaves.
With meat. Mix pulp with minced or finely chopped cooked meat or poultry, add seasoning, little mayonnaise if wished.
With cheese. Mix pulp with grated cheese and mayonnaise.

Tomato quickies

Tomatoes on toast. Fried tomatoes to serve on toast should be well seasoned with salt and pepper and a good pinch of sugar.

Tomatoes au gratin. Sliced tomatoes, put into a shallow dish, seasoned and topped with breadcrumbs, grated cheese and margarine, then cooked under the grill or in the oven are delicious with fish, cold ham or an omelette.
Tomato salad. Slice tomatoes, add little oil and vinegar, chopped parsley, chopped chives and seasoning. Leave for an hour or so and serve in a salad, or as an hors-d'oeuvre.
Tomatoes Italienne. Halve 6 large tomatoes. Chop contents of a small tin of anchovies, mix with 2 hard-boiled eggs, 2 oz. breadcrumbs, little chopped parsley and seasoning and the oil from the anchovy fillets. Pile on the tomatoes. Top with little margarine or butter and bake for about 8 minutes in a hot oven (450°F.—Gas Mark 7).

Tomato toasts

Cooking time   10 minutes

You will need:

4 large tomatoes	1 small onion
4 oz. chopped ham or cooked meat	2 oz. margarine (or butter)
4 large slices buttered toast	2 eggs
	seasoning
	parsley

1 Slice tomatoes, skinning them if wished.
2 Chop onion and cook in hot margarine then add ham or meat, the tomatoes and cook all together until very soft.
3 Add beaten eggs, seasoning and continue cooking until eggs are very lightly set.
4 Pile on to hot pieces of toast and garnish with parsley.
5 This makes an excellent quick supper dish.

Tomato pie

Cooking time   1 hour

You will need:

2 large onions	3–4 oz. breadcrumbs
2 oz. butter	salt and pepper
1 lb. tomatoes	4 eggs

1 Peel the onions and put them into a bowl of boiling water and leave them there for 2 or 3 hours. This is not essential, but it does mean they cook more quickly and have a lovely transparent appearance.
2 Drain, dry and slice them and fry them lightly in butter.
3 Butter a fireproof dish and fill it with alternate layers of the onions and sliced peeled tomatoes, sprinkling each layer with a few breadcrumbs, seasoned with salt and pepper.
4 Finish with a good layer of the crumbs, dot with flakes of butter and bake in a moderate oven for about 1 hour (375°F.—Gas Mark 4).
5 Top with poached eggs.

Bacon and beef patties

Cooking time   30 minutes

You will need:

8 oz. short crust pastry (see page 86)	3 rashers bacon – streaky bacon can be used for these
8 oz. minced or chopped cooked or flaked corned beef	1 egg
½–1 teaspoon mixed herbs (use the smaller quantity if using dried herbs)	2 skinned and chopped tomatoes
	seasoning
	milk or a little egg

1 Roll out the pastry and cut into 8 rounds.
2 Chop the bacon and mix with all the other ingredients.
3 Put the mixture in the centre of 4 of the rounds.
4 Damp the edges of the pastry and put the other 4 rounds on top.
5 Seal the edges firmly and brush over the top with milk or a little egg.
6 Bake for approximately 25–30 minutes in the centre of a hot oven (450 °F. – Gas Mark 7), reducing the heat to moderate after the first 15 minutes.
7 Lift off the baking tin to cool.
8 To keep the pastry crisp remember to make a small air hole with the point of a knife before baking.
9 You can decorate the patties with leaves and a small tassel or rose of pastry.

Variations

Omit the tomatoes and add 2 oz. finely chopped mushrooms instead. Add a spoonful of chutney and a shake of curry powder to the mixture. Since the chutney makes the mixture more moist, use 2 small tomatoes only.

Baconburgers   *with curry sauce*

Cooking time   20 minutes

You will need:

4 slices bacon	½ teaspoon salt
1 lb. minced beef	¼ teaspoon garlic salt
⅛ teaspoon pepper	.2 tablespoons butter or margarine
sauce	
1 oz. flour	2 teaspoons curry powder
¼ teaspoon garlic salt	½ pint milk
¼ teaspoon salt	4 slices toast
1½ oz. butter or margarine	

1 Fry bacon until almost crisp.
2 Remove from pan and quickly curl each strip around the end of a wooden spoon.
3 Secure each with a tooth-pick.
4 Mix together the beef, pepper, salt and garlic salt.
5 Shape into 4 patties and sauté in the butter or margarine for 6 minutes.
6 For the sauce: Melt the butter or margarine in a saucepan.
7 Mix together the flour, curry powder, garlic salt and salt and thoroughly blend into the butter or margarine.
8 Gradually add milk, stirring until smooth.
9 Cook and stir until thickened and flavours blended.
10 Place each patty on a slice of toast.
11 Top with a bacon curl and pour sauce over each.

Beef cakes

Cooking time   8–10 minutes

You will need:

1 can corned beef	1 egg
approximately 8 oz. mashed potatoes	breadcrumbs to coat
	fat for frying

1 Mix the beef and potatoes together and season well. If rather dry add either an egg or milk to bind.
2 Form into cakes, coat with beaten egg and crumbs.
3 Fry until crisp and brown.
4 Serve with fried tomatoes, mushrooms etc.

Beef pancakes

Cooking time   12 minutes

You will need:

for the batter

4 oz. flour	½ pint milk and water
1 egg	fat for frying
pinch salt	

for the filling

2 thinly sliced onions	2 rashers bacon
seasoning	1 can finely chopped corned beef
2 oz. margarine	
2 sliced tomatoes	4 tablespoons milk

1 First make batter by sieving flour and salt together, then add egg and a little of the liquid.
2 Beat very hard.
3 Gradually add rest of liquid and beat until batter is smooth.
4 Now prepare the filling by frying onions and tomatoes in margarine.
5 Add chopped bacon and cook until crisp.
6 Add corned beef, milk, seasoning and heat thoroughly.
7 Heat a small knob of fat in frying pan, pour a little of batter in this and cook until golden, toss or turn pancake and cook until brown on under side.
8 Slide on to a hot plate, cover with a layer of filling. Keep pancake hot by putting plate over saucepan of hot water.
9 Continue cooking pancakes and pile on top of each other with a layer of filling between each.
10 Fry tomatoes or mushrooms to garnish.
11 To serve, cut into 4 thick slices.

Casserole of sausage and corn

Cooking time   20 minutes

You will need:

8 small sausages	salt and pepper
can corn	½ pint white sauce
½ green pepper, chopped	(see page 21)

1 Mix corn, green pepper, salt and pepper.
2 Place in casserole in alternate layers with white sauce.
3 Arrange sausages on top to radiate from centre.
4 Bake in moderate oven for 20 minutes (375 °F. – Gas Mark 4).

Corn and bacon fritters

Cooking time   5–15 minutes

You will need:

1 small size carton frozen sweet corn, or can of corn	2 rashers bacon
	2 oz. self-raising flour
	fat for frying
⅛ pint milk (½ gill)	

1 Cook the corn according to the directions on the carton if using frozen variety. The canned variety should just be strained.
2 Cut the rashers of bacon into small dice.
3 Fry gently for a few minutes.
4 Remove from the pan.
5 Make a batter with the flour and milk.
6 Stir in the corn and bacon.
7 Heat a little more fat in the frying pan and fry tablespoons of the mixture, turning once, until golden brown on both sides, about 5 minutes.

Corned beef fritters

Cooking time   10 minutes

You will need:

1 can corned beef	seasoning
2 oz. flour	little chopped parsley or
1 or 2 beaten eggs	grated onion to flavour
1 gill milk	fat for frying

1 Open tin of corned beef, flake the meat.
2 Beat flour with eggs and milk and add meat etc.
3 Drop spoonfuls of the mixture into the hot fat, turning when crisp and brown.

Corned beef hamburgers

Cooking time   10 minutes

You will need:

1 can corned beef	2 chopped gherkins
1 teaspoon mustard	4 large or 8 small rolls
lettuce	tomatoes
watercress	butter
1 tablespoon mustard pickle	

1 Chop the corned beef and mix with the chopped gherkins, chopped pickles and mustard.
2 Split and butter the rolls, spread with the corned beef mixture, then brush the outside of the rolls with a little butter.
3 Put into a fairly hot oven for about 10 minutes.
4 Meanwhile make a salad of lettuce, watercress and tomatoes.

Corned beef cakes

Cooking time   12 minutes

You will need:

1 can corned beef	1 tablespoon grated onion
1 egg	2 tablespoons bread-crumbs
seasoning	
fat for frying	fried tomatoes and fried bread to garnish
1 tablespoon chopped parsley	

1 Flake the meat and mix with other ingredients.
2 Heat a little fat in frying pan.
3 Fry bread and halved tomatoes and keep warm in oven.
4 Drop spoonfuls corned beef mixture into fat.
5 Fry on 1 side, turn carefully and brown other side.
6 Serve at once.

Frankfurter rolls

Cooking time   15 minutes

You will need:

4 bridge rolls	4 large or 8 small
4 tomatoes	frankfurter sausages
seasoning	mustard
butter	cress

1 Split and butter the rolls.
2 Slice the tomatoes thickly and spread the slices over the bottom halves of the rolls.
3 Split the frankfurters and spread with made mustard, put on to the tomato slices and cover with the buttered tops of rolls.
4 Wrap in greaseproof paper or, better still, aluminium foil, and bake for about 15 minutes in a moderatley hot oven (425 °F. – Gas Mark 6).
5 Unwrap and serve at once with cress.

Crispy ham roll-ups

No cooking time except boiling eggs

You will need:

3 oz. coarsely crushed cheese biscuits	2 hard-boiled eggs
1 tablespoon chopped green peppers or 1 tablespoon chopped gherkins	1 teaspoon grated onion
	1 tablespoon chopped parsley
	pinch of salt
8 oz. sliced boiled ham (6 or 7 slices)	$\frac{1}{4}$ cup mayonnaise
	2 teaspoons prepared mustard

1 Chop eggs.
2 Blend crumbs with finely chopped eggs, onion, parsley, green pepper, salt and mayonnaise.
3 Spread each ham slice with mustard, then with biscuit crumb stuffing and roll up.
4 Serve with olives or gherkins.

Double decker Creole

Cooking time   5 minutes

You will need:

3 slices buttered toast, each cut across in 2 triangles

top layer filling

4 slices liver sausage spread lightly with mustard, warmed under	grill and topped with 1 tablespoon finely chopped fried onion

bottom layer – Hot Slaw

3 oz. finely shredded cabbage boiled for 1 minute in 2 tablespoons vinegar then drained	a sprinkling of salt 1 teaspoon butter 1 teaspoon brown sugar

1 Sandwich buttered toast together with fillings.
2 Press down well, cutting across again, if liked.
3 Garnish with slices of tomato and pickled gherkin.
Note: Fillings for hot sandwiches vary according to taste, hunger, mood and what there is in the pantry. Cheese, eggs, canned fish and meats, peanut butter, pickles and relishes make interesting combinations for hot layer sandwiches. Seasonings are important and a salad accompaniment makes this type of snack a balanced meal.

Griddle cakes
with sausages and bacon

Cooking time   4–5 minutes

You will need for 12–14 cakes:

8 oz. self-raising flour	$\frac{1}{2}$ level teaspoon salt
$\frac{1}{2}$ pint milk	1 egg

1 Sift flour and salt together into a mixing bowl.

2 Make a well in the centre and add the milk and beaten egg and stir just until smooth.
3 Pour batter from the tip of a large spoon on to a lightly greased hot griddle, heavy frying pan or hot plate of an electric cooker.
4 Cook until bubbles begin to form on the surface, then turn and brown on the other side.
5 Serve warm with butter, sausages and bacon.
6 These are delicious also with fried tomatoes and bacon.

Ham soufflé

Cooking time   25–35 minutes

You will need for 2–3 servings:

$\frac{1}{4}$ pint thick white sauce (see page 21)	parsley to garnish
4 oz. finely chopped ham	4 eggs
	seasoning

1 Separate the eggs.
2 Blend egg yolks into sauce.
3 Add ham and seasoning and fold in stiffly beaten egg whites.
4 Pour into a prepared soufflé dish and bake in a moderate oven (375°F.—Gas Mark 4) for 25–35 minutes.
5 Serve at once, garnished with parsley.

Ham and tomato mould

Cooking time   few minutes

You will need:

8 oz. cooked ham	4 hard-boiled eggs
seasoning	$\frac{1}{2}$ pint tomato juice
1 or 2 oz. cream or cottage cheese	1 dessertspoon powder gelatine

1 Dissolve the powder gelatine in the very hot tomato juice, softening it first in a tablespoon water.
2 When cold, but not set, stir in 2 sliced hard-boiled eggs and the diced ham.
3 Put into a rinsed mould and allow to set.
4 Turn out and serve on a bed of lettuce.
5 Halve the other 2 hard-boiled eggs, take out the centre yolk, mash, season and mix with a little cream cheese.
6 Pile back into the white cases and cut into quarters, so you have 8 portions, and arrange these round the mould.

Hot bacon and oat cobbler

Cooking time   25 minutes

You will need for 4–6 servings:

1 or 2 cans concentrated vegetable soup	3–4 rashers bacon
2 oz. butter or margarine	6 oz. self-raising flour
salt and pepper to taste	2 oz. rolled oats
little grated cheese	1 egg
	milk to make ¼ pint with the egg

1 Cut bacon into small pieces and fry.
2 Sieve flour and seasonings into basin.
3 Add rolled oats.
4 Mix thoroughly.
5 Rub margarine in lightly.
6 Add bacon.
7 Beat egg and milk together.
8 Pour over dry ingredients.
9 Mix with palette knife.
10 Roll out on floured board to about ¼ inch thick. Cut into rounds.
11 Put the vegetable soup into a casserole and meanwhile heat for about 10 minutes in a moderately hot oven (400°F.—Gas Mark 5).
12 Arrange rounds of scone on top, sprinkle with grated cheese to give them an attractive glaze.
13 Bake for approximately 12–15 minutes in a hot oven (425–450°F.—Gas Mark 6–7). This makes a filling and economical meal.

Macaroni Valetta

Cooking time   15 minutes

You will need:

4–6 oz. quick-cooking macaroni	½–¾ pint white sauce (depending on amount of macaroni used) (see page 21)
3–4 sliced tomatoes	
3–4 oz. ham or corned beef	
1 oz. fat	3–4 oz. mushrooms cut in large slices

1 Put macaroni in boiling salted water.
2 Cook for 7 minutes.
3 Meanwhile heat fat in frying pan and cook mushrooms, then the tomatoes.
4 Make white sauce and, when boiled and quite smooth, heat chopped ham in this.
5 Drain macaroni, mix with sauce and fried mushrooms.
6 Pile into hot dish and decorate with fried tomatoes.
7 Spaghetti may be used instead of macaroni in this recipe.

Minced ham with eggs

Cooking time   10 minutes

You will need:

4 eggs	2–3 tablespoons chopped parsley
1 onion	seasoning
1–2 tablespoons tomato purée	stick celery
2 oz. butter	4–6 oz. minced or chopped ham

1 Trim and cut 1 large onion and a small stick of celery into cubes.
2 Fry in butter or margarine until tender.
3 Mix with the ham, add chopped parsley and tomato purée.
4 Put into individual ovenproof dishes, break an egg in the middle of each and bake in a moderate oven (375°F.—Gas Mark 4) for about 10 minutes, until the eggs are set.

Party platter

Cooking time   10 minutes to boil eggs

You will need:

4 eggs (hard-boil these in the morning, if possible)	mayonnaise
	4 slices ham
	4 slices tongue
little anchovy essence	about 2 oz. cream cheese
chicory	chutney
tomatoes	lettuce
gherkins	grated carrot

1 Mix the grated carrot with cream cheese, spread over the slices of ham and roll firmly.
2 Halve the eggs, mix the yolks with anchovy essence and mayonnaise and pile back into whites.
3 Spread the slices of tongue with chutney and chopped gherkins and roll.
4 Separate the pieces of chicory and fill with cream cheese.
5 Arrange all these on bed of lettuce and garnish with sliced tomatoes

Ragoût of kidney and tomatoes

Cooking time   approximately 20 minutes

You will need:

4 lambs' kidneys	4 large tomatoes
1 green pepper	2 oz. butter
seasoning	little flour
about ½ gill stock	1 gill red wine
large onion	shake paprika pepper

1 Slice the onion and green pepper.
2 Halve the kidneys and roll in seasoned flour, then fry gently in the butter.
3 Add the onions and pepper and cook for about 5 minutes.
4 Put in the sliced tomatoes, wine, stock and more seasoning and cook until tender.

Rice cutlets

Cooking time   15 minutes

You will need:

2 teaspoons grated onion	crisp breadcrumbs
2 teaspoons chopped parsley	¼ pint thick white sauce (see page 21)
4 oz. cooked rice	seasoning
6–8 oz. cooked minced meat	1 tablespoon melted butter or margarine
	brown or paprika sauce

1 Mix all ingredients but melted butter and crumbs together.
2 Form into cutlet shapes, brush lightly with butter, roll in crumbs.
3 Cook under grill until crisp. Turn and brown on the other side.
4 Serve with a good brown or paprika sauce. This is made by adding 1–2 teaspoons paprika pepper to ½ pint white sauce.

Sausage and egg galantine

Cooking time   55 minutes

You will need:

1 lb. sausage meat	pinch mixed herbs
2 or 3 hard-boiled eggs	1 beaten egg
little seasoned flour	few crisp breadcrumbs

1 Work half the egg and the herbs into the sausage meat.
2 Put flour on your pastry board and roll out sausage meat to a neat rectangle.
3 Put the hard-boiled eggs on this.
4 Roll firmly.
5 Brush with remainder of the egg and coat with breadcrumbs.
6 Bake for 45 minutes in a moderate oven (375°F. – Gas Mark 4).
7 Serve hot or cold.
8 Instead of sausage meat you could use 12 oz. minced beef mixed with 4 oz. breadcrumbs and seasoning.

Savoury kidneys

Cooking time   10–15 minutes

You will need:

4 slices of bread	4 small rashers of bacon
butter	little butter
small amount of flour	seasoning
4 lambs' kidneys	2 tomatoes

1 Cut kidneys into small pieces and roll in seasoned flour.
2 Chop up bacon and fry lightly, add a little butter, then fry the kidneys and skinned sliced tomatoes until kidneys are soft.
3 Pile on hot buttered toast and garnish with parsley or serve on bed of cooked rice and serve with salad or peas.

Savoury beef mixture

If you have a cool larder or a refrigerator a good saucepan of a savoury minced beef mixture can be used in a number of ways but *never* attempt to keep this too long if you haven't a cool storage space.

You will need:

3 oz. fat	tube tomato purée
3 good sized onions	(small size)
3 oz. flour	can of tomatoes
2 lb. minced beef	seasoning
	stock of water

1 Heat the fat and fry the finely chopped or grated onions then work in the flour and cook for several minutes.
2 Add the tomato purée, can tomatoes and 1 pint of stock or water flavoured with yeast or meat extract.
3 Bring to the boil, season well, then add the minced beef.
4 Stir well to break up the meat then simmer gently for about 1 hour.

To batch No. 1. Serve as a hot sauce with cooked rice or spaghetti or vegetables. Use a good ¼ of this for 4 people.

To batch No. 2. Take about ¼ of this, add 4 oz. soft breadcrumbs, little mixed herbs and chopped parsley. Work together well and form into a loaf shape. Serve with salad. The loaf will slice if well chilled.

To batch No. 3. Cut the tops off tomatoes, scoop out the centre, pulp, mix with ¼ of the meat mixture. Pile this back into the tomato cases. Either bake for 15 minutes and serve hot with mixed vegetables or serve cold, topped with mayonnaise and garnished with salad.

To batch No. 4. Use the remaining ¼ for lining 4 scallop shells, making a hollow in the centre. Break an egg into each, season well and if liked top with grated cheese. Bake for 15 minutes in a moderate oven (375 °F. – Gas Mark 4). Serve with freshly buttered rolls and salad.

Spiced patties

Cooking time   10 minutes

You will need:

8 oz. minced rump steak	1 clove of crushed garlic or use 1 tablespoon of chopped chives
1 finely chopped onion	2 teaspoons Worcestershire sauce
2 teaspoons capers	pepper and salt
2 teaspoons chopped parsley	soft breadcrumbs
egg	fat for frying
tomatoes	
8 oz. beef or pork sausage meat	

1 Mix all the ingredients together, except egg and breadcrumbs.
2 Form into 8 patties.
3 Coat with egg and soft breadcrumbs.
4 Fry steadily in shallow hot fat.
5 Drain well. Serve hot on halved tomatoes.

Spanish potatoes

Cooking time   15 minutes

You will need:

1 tablespoon minced onion	½ teaspoon paprika
2 tablespoons chopped green pepper	3 oz. fat
	4 diced boiled potatoes
4 oz. chopped cooked ham	1 teaspoon salt

1 Sauté onion, pepper, in fat until light brown.
2 Add potatoes, ham and seasonings and cook until heated through.

Southern luncheon bake

Cooking time   20 minutes

You will need:

4 ½-inch slices ham	½ teaspoon salt
whole cloves	8 oz. mashed cooked potatoes
6 canned pineapple rings	1 teaspoon grated orange peel
2 tablespoons cranberry sauce or red currant jelly	1 gill orange juice
2 tablespoons butter, melted	1 tablespoon brown sugar

1 Arrange ham slices in shallow baking dish, stud sides with cloves.
2 Place a pineapple ring on each ham slice.
3 Beat butter and salt into potatoes and mount on pineapple rings.
4 Brown in oven 20 minutes (375 °F. – Gas Mark 4).
5 In saucepan, combine cranberry sauce, orange peel, juice and brown sugar.
6 Heat the ingredients together and serve separately.

Tongue and cream cheese rolls

No cooking time

You will need:

4 good-sized slices of tongue	French dressing (see page 63)
2 tablespoons chopped cucumber	3 oz. soft cream cheese
1 teaspoon chopped spring onion	2 teaspoons capers
	little well-flavoured chutney or piccalilli

to garnish

cooked peas	potato salad
beetroot	

1 Spread each slice of tongue with chutney.
2 Mix the cheese, cucumber, onion and capers together.
3 Moisten with a very little French dressing.
4 Put on to the slices of tongue and roll, making sure the light filling shows at either end of each roll.
5 Arrange in a ring of sliced beetroot and garnish with potato salad and peas.

Chapter 6   Snacks and Salads

In this chapter you will find a number of suggestions for delicious sandwiches, and other quick savouries, good enough to be served when you entertain, easy enough to solve all your problems when a hurried snack is required.

Your will also find a number of time-saving practical suggestions for the making of salads and some excellent salad recipes.

20 different savoury snacks

Cooking time   5–15 minutes

Toasted snacks are so easy and can be extremely appetising as well. They can be anything from a main meal to a dainty titbit to tempt the appetite.

Toast bread under a hot grill or in a toaster, or, where possible, over a red-hot coal fire.
Trim the crusts if preferred. Butter well, and keep hot while making the topping.

1 Scrambled eggs: Beat the eggs, allowing 1 per person, season well, and for a softer mixture add 1 tablespoon milk to each 2 eggs. Heat a knob of butter in the pan and pour in the mixture. Cook as slowly as possible, stirring all the time until lightly set. Remove from heat while still a little liquid, since the eggs will stiffen slightly in the pan.

2 Scrambled eggs with chicken: Heat any tiny scraps of cooked chicken in the milk and butter, then add the beaten seasoned egg and cook as before.

3 Scrambled eggs with ham: As with chicken, but as ham is slightly salt, reduce quantity in seasoning.

4 Scrambled eggs with tomatoes: Allow a good-sized tomato for each 2 eggs. Skin and slice thinly and heat in the butter. Beat eggs, add to milk, season and cook as before.

5 Scrambled eggs with bacon, macaroni or spaghetti: Fry the bacon in the pan until really crisp, then add the cooked and well-drained macaroni. Heat for a minute, add the eggs and cook as before.

6 Scrambled eggs with fried bread and onions: Chop an onion finely and cook in the hot butter until soft then add a few cubes of bread and brown these. Add the beaten eggs and cook as before.

7 Tomatoes on toast: Halve or slice the tomatoes and fry steadily in butter or margarine. Season and add pinch sugar to taste. Garnish with chopped parsley, or serve with crisp bacon or poached or fried eggs on top.

8 English monkey: For 4 slices of toast. Heat 1 oz. butter in pan, add 1 gill milk, 2 oz. soft breadcrumbs. When very hot add 2 oz. grated cheese and a beaten egg. Season well, adding little made mustard and few drops Worcestershire sauce. Stir together until thick and creamy. Pour on to toast, garnish with sliced tomato.

9 Cheese and apple rings: Peel and core apples. Fry thick rings of apple in bacon fat. When apples are soft, add a slice of cheese and leave until beginning to melt. Put both apple and cheese slices on to toast.

10 Creamed haddock: Heat a good knob of butter in a pan, add little milk and flaked, cooked, smoked haddock. Heat together until a thick mixture. If wished, a beaten egg can be stirred into the mixture. Garnish with paprika pepper.

11 Roes on toast: Either fry the soft roes in hot butter or cook in milk and butter in a pan or on a dish over hot water. Drain well and garnish with paprika pepper.

12 Cod's roes: Cut the cooked cod's roe into slices and fry steadily in butter or, better still, use bacon fat, until pale golden brown. Put on to hot toast with a fried bacon rasher.

13 Kidneys on toast: Skin and halve the kidneys, season well and fry in hot butter until tender. OR quarter kidneys, coat in well-seasoned flour. Fry chopped bacon in a pan, add a little butter then the kidneys and cook steadily, adding little water or port wine to moisten. Excellent topped with a poached egg.

14 Poached eggs: Crack each egg, pour into a saucer. Season lightly. Butter a cup or poacher well and heat before pouring in the egg. Eggs can be poached in a special poacher, or in a cup in a pan of water, or lower the eggs into boiling water in a pan. When set, lift on to hot buttered toast.

15 Poached eggs with Welsh rarebit: Top Welsh rarebit or toasted cheese with a poached egg.

16 Poached eggs with mushrooms: Fry sliced mushrooms in hot butter, pile on toast then top with a poached egg.

17 Poached eggs in cheese sauce: Put the poached eggs on buttered toast, cover with a cheese sauce, sprinkle with grated cheese and brown very quickly under a hot grill.

18 Sardines on toast: Arrange well-drained sardines on hot buttered toast, season lightly, and heat for a minute under the grill.

19 Sardines on toast with tomatoes: Mash sardines, season well and spread on buttered toast. Cover with thickly sliced, skinned tomatoes, brush with little butter and cook under medium grill.

20 Sardines with cheese on toast: Mash sardines, season well and spread on toast. Cover with grated cheese and brown under the grill.

10 Savoury spreads for toast or sandwiches

1 Grated cheese, grated carrot and little chopped parsley, mixed together with mayonnaise.
2 Creamed butter, chopped watercress and a squeeze of lemon juice, seasoned well.
3 Creamed cheese and finely chopped celery; use a small amount of the green leaves too.
4 Creamed cheese and chopped boiled bacon or ham, then just a touch of chutney.
5 Chopped hard-boiled eggs, crisp chopped bacon and little mayonnaise to bind.
6 Chopped soft-boiled eggs, knob butter, little chopped parsley or watercress, pinch celery, salt and seasoning.
7 Chopped hard-boiled eggs, pinch curry powder and a little chutney.
8 Chopped tongue, chopped beetroot and little mayonnaise to bind.
9 Smoked cooked haddock, chopped lettuce and chopped gherkin. Bind together with butter.
10 Flaked cooked kippers (be careful to take out all the bones) little butter, squeeze of lemon juice and lots of pepper.

Toasted snacks under the grill

Cooking time   5–10 minutes

Toast 2 slices of bread for each person, butter. Meanwhile grill rashers of bacon (thin). Sandwich together and serve at once.
or put a slice of cheese on top of bacon rashers. Add chutney if wished.
or fill sandwich with grilled filleted herring or kipper.
or with mashed sardines. Spread over 1 slice of toast and heat for 1 minute then top with 2nd slice.
or with lean ham, heated for 1 minute under grill.
or with sliced or grated cheese mixed with chopped gherkins. Spread on 1 slice of toast, heat for 1 minute then top with second slice.
or butter bread and cover with a generous layer of beef paste. Roll each slice very firmly. Brush with melted butter or margarine and either crisp under a hot grill or in the oven. Other varieties of pastes can be used instead.

Fried hot sandwiches

Cooking time   5 minutes

Cheese dreams. Make sandwiches of bread and butter and your favourite cheese. Cut into fingers and fry until crisp and brown.

Croque monsieur. This is a slightly more sophisticated version of the cheese dreams. Cut slices of bread and butter (French bread is ideal for this), sandwich with sliced Gruyère cheese and ham and fry as before.

Supper sandwich

Cooking time   6 minutes

You will need for 1–2 servings:
1 Butter 4–5 slices of toast.
2 Place a layer of processed cheese on each.
3 Grill until cheese melts.
4 Heat 1 can tomato soup seasoned with 1 tablespoon chopped pickle.
5 Pour on sandwiches.

Three-decker club sandwich

Cooking time   5 minutes

You will need for 1–2 servings:

3 slices buttered toast	1 slice boiled bacon or
1 oz. Cheddar cheese	ham
lettuce	mayonnaise
tomato	made mustard

1 Season mayonnaise with mustard.
2 On large slice of toast put sliced or minced boiled bacon or ham, moistened with a little mayonaise.
3 Top with second slice of toast, then with sliced or grated cheese, moisten with mayonnaise.
4 Top with third slice of toast.
5 Work quickly so that the toast is still warm when served.
6 Cut across and serve with lettuce and tomato.

Swiss toasts

Cooking time   5–10 minutes

You will need:	
4 slices cheese	4 slices lean ham or other
4 slices bread	cold meat
1 large tomato	little margarine
	chutney

1 Toast the bread lightly, spread with a little margarine.
2 Put ham on each piece of toast, spreading it lightly with chutney.
3 Top with a cheese slice and a ring of tomato.

Put into a moderately hot oven (400°F.—Gas Mark 5) for 10 minutes until cheese just starts to melt.
Serve at once with crisp watercress.

Mock pizza pie

Cooking time   30 minutes

You will need:

4 large slices of bread	little fat
1 can tomatoes	1 large onion
few olives or parsley	can sardines or
grated cheese	anchovies

1 Brush the large slices of bread with fat and arrange on a dish.
2 Fry the onions until tender, mix with the tomatoes and arrange on the bread.
3 Top with grated cheese and brown in the oven.
4 Garnish with anchovies or sardines and olives or parsley.

Mock vol-au-vent cases

Cooking time   10 minutes

Made of bread, these cases are an excellent substitute for puff pastry and, of course, far less trouble.
Cut slices of bread about $\frac{3}{4}$ inch thick, cut in rounds with pastry cutter.
With a small cutter, take a circle from centre of each, removing only about $\frac{1}{4}$ inch in thickness of the bread.
Fry until crisp and golden in hot butter or vegetable shortening.
Drain well and fill with savoury mixtures.

Easy savoury fillings:

Scrambled egg and grated cheese.
Thick cheese sauce and grated RAW carrot.
Chopped fried mushrooms.
Fried onions, tomatoes and chopped anchovies.
Left over meat, fish etc. in thick sauce.

Vol-au-vent cases

and fillings

Cooking time   15 minutes

You may not have time to do much baking so why not either buy ready-baked pastry cases or the made puff pastry which just needs rolling out and baking. For hot weather, nothing is nicer than these, filled and served with a good salad. Try some of these fillings:
Cream cheese and chopped ham. Mix 2–3 oz. cream cheese with the same amount of cooked ham. Moisten with mayonnaise. Garnish with radish waterlilies.

Savoury tongue. Mix chopped tongue with finely chopped chutney and a little mayonnaise.
Spiced beef. Mix chopped, cooked or corned beef with mayonnaise, chopped spring onions and a little horseradish.
Scrambled egg and anchovies. Lightly scramble eggs, adding chopped anchovies just before eggs are set. Garnish with rolled anchovies.
Fish filling. Mix flaked, canned or shell fish with mayonnaise, chopped cucumber and capers.

Savoury tarts

Cooking time   15 minutes

You will need to make some small tartlets of short crust pastry (see page 86). When crisp and cold, fill with any of the following:
Chopped hard-boiled eggs mixed with mayonnaise and a little chopped gherkin, OR
Canned or flaked cooked fish mixed with thick mayonnaise, chopped gherkins, parsley and capers.
Garnish with rings of radishes, strips of parsley and hard-boiled egg.

Savoury triangles

Cooking time   5 minutes for scrambled eggs

You will need:

6 large square slices of buttered white bread	3 large square slices of buttered brown bread
3 eggs	2 oz. ham
6 oz. soft cream cheese	2 large tomatoes
seasoning	about 2 inches cucumber
few olives	tiny piece gherkin or
knob of butter	spring onion

1 Slice the tomatoes and cucumber thinly and season well.
2 Heat the knob of butter, beat and season the eggs and scramble lightly, adding the chopped ham.
3 Spread 3 of the slices of white bread and butter with the ham and egg mixture, cover with the brown slice.
4 Top this with the sliced tomatoes and cucumber, then the other white slices.
5 Beat the cream cheese until it is very soft, if necessary add a few drops of milk.
6 Cut each of the 3 large sandwich squares into 4 triangles—making 12 in all.
7 Coat top and sides with thin cheese, rather like icing little cakes.
8 Garnish on top with the slices of olive and leaves of gherkins or spring onions.

Welsh rarebit

Cooking time   5–10 minutes

You will need:

4–6 large slices of toast	butter for toast
8 oz. cheese	salt
1 teaspoon made mustard	pepper
	1 oz. butter
1 tablespoon beer or ale or Worcestershire sauce	1 oz. flour
	½ pint milk

1 Heat the butter in a saucepan, stir in the flour and cook steadily for several minutes, then gradually add the cold milk.
2 Bring to the boil and cook until smooth and thick.
3 Add the mustard, salt, pepper, most of the cheese and the beer.
4 Heat steadily, without boiling too quickly, until the cheese has melted.
5 Spread over the hot buttered toast, sprinkle with the remainder of the cheese and brown under a hot grill.
6 Serve at once.

SNACKS WITH FISH

Breton fingers

Cooking time   10 minutes

You will need:

1 small can sardines in oil	2 oz. grated Cheddar cheese
½ teaspoon made mustard	seasoning
4 slices buttered toast	little margarine, or butter if necessary
1 teaspoon Worcestershire sauce	1 tomato
	1 heaped tablespoon breadcrumbs

1 Mash the sardines very well and season.
2 Mix the oil from the tin of sardines with the breadcrumbs, seasoning, Worcestershire sauce and cheese.
3 If there is not sufficient oil to give a soft mixture then add a little margarine or butter and cream well.
4 Spread the mashed sardines on the slices of toast and cover with the crumb mixture.
5 Put under a hot grill for a few minutes until crisp and golden brown.
6 Garnish with a small piece of tomato and serve hot or cold.
7 If serving hot the fingers can be prepared earlier and just heated in oven.

Mushroom and haddock fillets

Cooking time   10–15 minutes

You will need:

4–6 oz. quick cooking macaroni	2 oz. butter
1 good dessertspoon chopped parsley	4 thin fillets of fresh haddock (about 3 oz. each)
1 can condensed mushroom soup	¼ can milk

1 Place haddock in frying pan.
2 Heat soup and milk in pan, pour over fish.
3 Cook gently for 7–10 minutes.
4 Meanwhile cook macaroni for 7 minutes in boiling salted water, drain.
5 Melt margarine in saucepan, add macaroni and parsley.
6 Mix, heat thoroughly.
7 Place in serving dish, top with fish and sauce.

Neapolitan macaroni

Cooking time   25 minutes

You will need:

2 onions	4–6 oz. macaroni
2 oz. margarine	small can anchovies or sardines
little grated cheese	
1 lb. tomatoes	

1 Fry grated onion in the margarine until very soft.
2 Add the sliced tomatoes and simmer gently for 15 minutes.
3 Cook the macaroni in boiling salted water until tender.
4 Add to the tomato mixture.
5 When hot, add the can of anchovies or sardines.
6 Pile on to dish and garnish with grated cheese.
7 Serve with crisp toast.

Prawn cutlets

Cooking time   20 minutes

As egg and vegetable cutlets (see page 39) but use chopped prawns with a little anchovy essence to flavour.

Scrambled kipper on toast

Cooking time   10 minutes

You will need:

4–8 kipper fillets— frozen or fresh	4 eggs
4 slices bread	2 tablespoons milk
2 oz. margarine or butter	very little salt
	pepper

1 Separate the kipper fillets and poach in water for 5 minutes.
2 When cooked, drain and flake the fish coarsely, removing the skin.
3 Break the eggs into a basin.
4 Add the milk and seasoning and beat lightly with a fork.
5 Meanwhile toast the bread, cut off crusts and spread with 1 oz. margarine.
6 Keep hot, melt the remaining ounce of margarine in a pan, add the eggs and cook gently, stirring occasionally.
7 When nearly set add the flaked kippers. Serve on toast.

MAKING A QUICK SALAD

A salad can be prepared in a very short time if you take advantage of the ready prepared or convenience foods available.

For green salads: It is time saving to wash and prepare lettuce, watercress etc. when purchased so they are all ready for use. Store them in the salad container or plastic bags in refrigerator or in a cool place.
Mustard and cress can often be purchased in containers, still growing, so cut and use as desired.
An unwashed lettuce keeps well in a biscuit tin or covered saucepan.
To prepare lettuce etc., in a hurry, wash in cold water, lay flat on tea towels and pat gently until dry, or shake well in salad container.

For Russian salads: Use the frozen prepared vegetables and cook as directed, drain well then toss in mayonnaise while still hot.
Canned Russian salad is a good standby. Top with a little paprika pepper and/or chopped parsley.

Potato salad: This can be bought ready for use in a tin. It is improved by adding little extra seasoning.

Canned beans, peas, asparagus: These all add interest to salads and use sliced apples, oranges etc., which are very easily prepared and combine well with all salad ingredients.

Salad specials
No cooking time
Stuffed celery salad: Mix cheese spread with a little soft mayonnaise. Fill centre of celery stick with this and dust with paprika pepper.
Stuffed chicory salad: Mix diced ham and hard-boiled eggs with equal quantities of salad cream and tomato ketchup. Fill centres of chicory hearts, garnish with hard-boiled egg yolk.
Cheese and pineapple: Mix diced pineapple chunks and diced cheese with mayonnaise. Pile on crisp lettuce or endive.
Winter specials: Arrange *raw* cauliflower, shredded cabbage, sprouts, spinach, sliced peppers, grated raw swedes, carrots, parsnip, nuts, apples, bananas, pineapple on a huge plate or in a large divided hors-d'oeuvre dish.

Apple cheese salad
No cooking
You will need:

4 dessert apples	juice of 1 lemon
2 oz. chopped dates	4 oz. cream cheese
seasoning	2 oz. chopped walnuts

1 Core but do not peel apples.
2 Cut each apple in 3 thick slices and sprinkle with lemon juice.
3 Mix cheese with nuts and dates, season well.
4 Spread on slices of apple and garnish with whole nuts.

French bean salad
No cooking
1 Mix 1 lb. cooked French beans (seasoned and flavoured with little lemon juice) with 2 chopped hard-boiled eggs, 1 thinly sliced green pepper.
2 Pile on lettuce and sprinkle with grated cheese.

Grapefruit and prawn salad
No cooking
You will need:

2 grapefruit	lettuce
½ pint prawns	mayonnaise
sliced cucumber	

1 Halve grapefruit, remove sections of fruit and mix with mayonnaise and picked prawns (leaving 4 unpicked prawns for garnish).
2 Shred a little lettuce, put at bottom of grapefruit cases, pile prawn mixture on top.
3 Garnish with sliced cucumber and unpicked prawns.

Lettuce cups with salmon

No cooking time

You will need:

8 leaves from the heart of the lettuce	1 small can salmon
mayonnaise	2 or 3 hard-boiled eggs
cucumber	little horseradish cream

1 Arrange the lettuce leaves on a dish.
2 Chop the egg yolks and whites separately.
3 Put a spoonful of salmon in the middle of each lettuce leaf, with a ring of egg yolk round, then a ring of egg white.
4 Blend the horseradish with a little mayonnaise and put on the salmon.
5 Serve with thinly sliced cucumber.

Harlequin salad

Cooking time   10 minutes

You will need for 4–6 servings:

6 oz. quick-cooking macaroni	little mustard
4 hard-boiled eggs	mayonnaise
3 oz. chopped ham or shelled shrimps	4 tomatoes
1 green pepper	small piece of cucumber or few chopped gherkins
lettuce	watercress
little chopped parsley	lemon

1 Cook macaroni for 7 minutes in boiling salted water.
2 Rinse macaroni under cold water, allow to dry.
3 Blend a little mustard with mayonnaise and toss macaroni in this.
4 Add chopped eggs, ham or shrimps, 2 of the tomatoes, sliced rather thickly, the diced cucumber and pepper.
5 Pile on a bed of lettuce and garnish with watercress, parsley, tomato and lemon.

Oriental chicken and rice salad

Cooking time   15–20 minutes

You will need for 3–4 servings:

6 oz. long grained rice	3 tablespoons salad oil
1 tablespoon vinegar, wine or tarragon for preference	salt and pepper to taste
	1 green pepper, finely sliced
1 tablespoon currants	
1 large tomato, skinned de-seeded and chopped	2 tablespoons chopped walnuts (optional)
	8 oz. cooked chicken cut into bite-size pieces
cut clove of garlic (optional)	

1 Cook rice until just tender in plenty of fast boiling, well salted water, then drain very thoroughly.
2 Meanwhile rub a large bowl with a cut clove of garlic and in it mix together the oil, vinegar and seasoning.
3 Add the hot rice and mix thoroughly.
4 Stir in the remaining ingredients and lastly the chicken.
5 Cover and set aside in a cool place for the flavours to blend.
6 When cold transfer to a serving dish.

Potato and bacon salad

Cooking time   30 minutes

You will need:

1 lb. new potatoes	1 tablespoon chopped parsley
2 or 3 rashers bacon	
French dressing	seasoning
1 tablespoon chopped onion	

1 Boil potatoes and fry bacon.
2 Dice and toss them with other ingredients while hot.
3 Serve on bed of lettuce when cold.

Sardine toadstools

Cooking time   10 minutes to hard-boil eggs

You will need:

4 hard-boiled eggs	2 firm tomatoes
can sardines	mayonnaise
lettuce	4 rounds bread and butter

1 Cut a fairly thick slice from each egg. It must be deep enough to enable you to remove the yolk without breaking the case.
2 Mash yolk with sardines. Season well and push back into white case.
3 Stand eggs on rounds of bread and butter.
4 Cut a slice off each end of the tomatoes. Balance this on the egg to make each look like a toadstool, put tiny dots of mayonnaise on top.
5 Arrange borders of lettuce round these, also using the 4 remaining slices of egg and the rest of the tomatoes.

Stuffed pear salad

No cooking

1 Peel, halve and core 4 dessert pears and toss in French dressing (see page 63).
2 Fill centres with cream cheese mixed with chopped glacé or fresh cherries.
3 Decorate with whole cherries and serve with watercress.

Summer salad

No cooking

1 Use an hors-d'oeuvre dish for a mixed salad.
2 In one section put potato salad garnished with rings of carrot, served on crisp lettuce.
3 In the second section, olives and carrots garnished with sliced carrot.
4 In the third a Russian salad.
5 In the fourth section, tiny beetroot.
6 Garnish each section with a 'waterlily' radish.

Summer platter

No cooking

You will need:

1 small lettuce	2 hard-boiled eggs
small piece cucumber	watercress
2 large tomatoes	↑banana
few radishes	1 orange
sliced strawberries	1 dessert apple
mayonnaise	few red or black currants
French dressing	chopped garlic or chives
garlic clove (optional)	

1 Toss lettuce and thinly sliced cucumber lightly in French dressing.
2 Cut radishes into slices or 'water lilies'.
3 Arrange lettuce on flat dish which can be lightly rubbed with a cut clove of garlic, if wished.
4 Arrange other ingredients in rows.
5 Serve with mayonnaise to which chopped garlic or chives have been added.

Surprise loaf

No cooking*

You will need:

1 sandwich loaf	4 oz. grated cheese
seasoning	4 oz. chopped cooked
2 skinned and chopped	ham or flaked corned
tomatoes	beef or finely chopped
¼ pint thick white sauce	cooked meat

*except for white sauce. (5–10 minutes) if serving cold, 35 minutes if serving hot (including white sauce).

1 Cut the crust off the loaf at 1 end, then scoop out the centre of the loaf.
2 This can be used for stuffings, or dried for breadcrumbs.
3 Mix all the ingredients together and press the moist filling into the centre of the loaf. Replace the crust.
4 If the weather is hot your family can just slice this stuffed loaf and eat it with salad. If cold,

then you need only to rub the outside of the loaf with a little margarine paper, put it into a moderately hot oven, together with a dish of sliced or whole seasoned tomatoes, and bake for about 25 minutes.
5 The size of the loaf depends on the fondness of your family for bread.

Tomato fish mould

Cooking time   15 minutes

You will need:

1 small can tomato soup	4 oz. flaked cooked fish or
or tomato juice	can of tuna fish or
2 hard-boiled eggs	salmon
seasoning	powder gelatine

1 Measure soup and to each ¼ pint allow 1 level dessertspoon powder gelatine (use slightly more gelatine with tomato juice as it is thinner than soup).
2 Dissolve gelatine in hot soup, add fish, sliced eggs and seasoning.
3 Pour into mould and allow to set.
4 Serve with salad.
5 For special occasions, add prawns to mould and garnish with prawns, whipped cream and cucumber. Serve with shredded lettuce.

Tomato and corned beef mould

Use the same recipe as tomato fish mould (see preceding recipe) but instead of the hard-boiled egg add sliced spring onions and 1 or 2 sliced gherkins or pieces of cucumber.

Tomato and salami salad

No cooking

1 Choose large, firm tomatoes.
2 Stand stalk side down and slice through nearly to the bottom 3 or 4 times.
3 Pack with slices of hard-boiled egg and salami.
4 Serve on a bed of cucumber, garnished with spring onions and served with mayonnaise.

Quick French dressing

No cooking

You will need:

6 tablespoons corn oil	3 tablespoons vinegar
seasoning	1 level tablespoon sugar

Put all ingredients into a screw-top jar and shake well.

Ways to flavour mayonnaise

Mayonnaise can form the basis of a number of new salad dressings; try the following:

Cheese mayonnaise: Cream 2 oz. soft cheese with 2 tablespoons milk. Add ¼ pint mayonnaise. Serve with vegetables, salads.

Curried mayonnaise: Blend 1–2 teaspoons curry powder with 1 or 2 tablespoons milk. Stir in ¼ pint mayonnaise. Serve with meat, salads.

Green mayonnaise: Add chopped fresh herbs to mayonnaise. Serve with fish salads, although if mint is used it is excellent with lamb salad.

Horseradish mayonnaise: Blend 1 tablespoon horseradish cream with ¼ pint mayonnaise. Serve with cold beef salad or canned salmon salad.

Lemon mayonnaise: Add grated rind and juice of 1 lemon to ¼ pint mayonnaise. Serve with cheese or fish salads.

Spiced mayonnaise: Add grated nutmeg and few drops Worcestershire sauce to ¼ pint mayonnaise. Serve with potato and vegetable salads.

Tomato mayonnaise: Add dessertspoon tomato ketchup or teaspoon tomato purée to ¼ pint mayonnaise. Serve with shell fish salad.

Chapter 7   Puddings and Sweets

Many families feel a meal is not complete without some kind of pudding or dessert. However, this need not be too much of a problem if you follow my suggestions in Chapter 1 for stocking your larder and make sure you always have a good supply of canned, packaged or frozen fruits and puddings on hand.

In the following chapter you will find a number of easy ideas for delicious but quick home-made desserts.

Puddings in minutes

Many of the quick cooking foods of today give puddings and sweets in a matter of minutes.

Custard and cornflour puddings: Make packet custard or cornflour as directed. Add chopped fruit, chopped nuts, fine biscuit crumbs or chopped chocolate.
Put into a dish and top with fruit. Serve at once or serve cold.

Fritters: A thick batter is mixed quickly with an efficient whisk. Coat fresh or well-drained canned fruit with this OR add dried fruit to the batter OR flavour it with spice or cinnamon or add desiccated coconut. Cook as directed (see fruit fritters, page 69) and top with coconut.

Pancakes: These give endless variety. Fill with jam, fruit, ice-cream.

Rice or macaroni puddings: Quick cooking or canned creamed rice or macaroni is a very easy pudding. Heat or cook as directed, tip into hot dish and top with coconut, or with brown sugar, and crisp under a moderately hot grill.

Sponge puddings: The variety of pudding and sponge mixtures available today are worth buying when short of time, for you can steam individual sponge puddings in 15 minutes, then top with jam or curd. Try covering drained canned or cooked fruit with one of the sponge mixtures, then bake for approximately 30 minutes in a moderate oven.

Jellied sweets: These take time to set—but are so little trouble to make that a number have been included in this chapter. A jelly will set in a much shorter time if you dissolve in $\frac{1}{4}$ pint boiling liquid only, then make up rest of liquid with cold water, milk, etc.

Almond cream

Cooking time   5–10 minutes (longer if using egg custard)

You will need:

$\frac{3}{4}$ pint thick custard – made with custard powder or yolks of 2 eggs and $\frac{3}{4}$ pint milk	3 average, sized macaroons, crumbled
	1 dessertspoon powdered gelatine
few drops almond essence	1 gill water
	2 oz. blanched almonds
	few glacé cherries

1 Dissolve the gelatine in the water.
2 Add to the hot custard, together with almond essence and macaroon crumbs.
3 Put into mould and allow to set.
4 Split the almonds and brown under a grill or in the oven.
5 Turn out the cream and decorate with almonds and cherries.

Almond pancakes

Cooking time   30 minutes

You will need:

$\frac{1}{2}$ pint pancake batter (see page 73)	fat or oil for cooking pancakes
3 oz. almonds	apricot jam or apple purée
1 egg white	1 oz. sugar.

1 Make and cook the pancakes wafer thin, in the usual way, but instead of rolling, spread each pancake with apple purée or jam and chopped almonds.
2 Pile on top of one another.
3 When the last pancake has been added, whisk egg white, fold in sugar.
4 Spread on top of the pancakes, sprinkle with nuts and brown in the oven, for 10 minutes.
5 Serve in slices like a cake.

'Baked' apples

Pressure cooking time   3 minutes

You will need:

large cooking apples	sugar to taste
$\frac{1}{4}$ pint water	

1 Wash the apples well and with a sharp knife slit the skin round the fruit.
2 Put a piece of greased paper over the rack or trivet and stand the apples on this.
3 Put in the water, fix the lid and bring *gradually* to pressure.
4 Lower the heat and cook for 3 minutes (preferably at 5 lb. pressure).
5 Be very careful the pressure does not get too high, otherwise the apples will become 'fluffy' on the outside before being cooked through to the middle.
6 Reduce pressure immediately.
7 The water at the bottom of the cooker has a very good flavour and could be thickened, sweetened and served as a sauce.

Poached apples and ginger

Cooking time   25 minutes

You will need:

4 medium-sized perfect cooking apples	2–3 oz. sugar
1–2 oz. crystallized ginger	$\frac{1}{2}$ pint water

1 Put sugar and water into pan, heat until sugar has dissolved, then add the chopped ginger.
2 Peel the apples, halve and core.
3 Poach apples in the hot ginger syrup until soft but unbroken. This means cooking them very slowly indeed with the lid off the pan so that the syrup thickens.
4 Put into sundae glasses and decorate with more pieces of ginger.

Apple crunch

Cooking time   40 minutes

You will need:

1 lb. apples	2 oz. butter or margarine
2 oz. dates	2 oz. sugar
little sugar to taste	4 oz. cornflakes
water	

1 Put sliced apples with dates, sugar and a very little water into dish and cook slowly until nearly tender and a thick mixture.
2 Cream butter and sugar, add cornflakes and press on top of apples.
3 Continue cooking in moderate oven (400 °F. – Gas Mark 4–5) until top is crisp.
4 Serve with cream or custard.
5 Do not have apples too juicy otherwise mixture on top will 'sink in'.
6 Any other fruit is equally good in this recipe and canned or bottled fruit can be used.

Banana blancmange

Cooking time   10 minutes

You will need:

1 packet vanilla- flavoured cornflour powder*	1 pint milk 1–2 oz. sugar 2 large or 3 small bananas

to decorate

little raspberry jam	sliced bananas

* or use $1\frac{1}{4}$ oz. plain cornflour and $\frac{1}{2}$ teaspoon vanilla essence.

1 Blend cornflour with a little cold milk.
2 Bring rest of milk to boil.
3 Pour over cornflour, return to pan and thicken, adding sugar.
4 When quite thick, add mashed bananas.
5 Allow to set.
6 Turn out.
7 Pour little jam on top and arrange rings of bananas just before serving.

Banana meringue

Cooking time   7 minutes

You will need:

1 packet chocolate- flavoured blancmange	cherries and angelica to decorate
4 sliced bananas	1 pint milk
2 eggs	3 tablespoons sugar

1 Blend blancmange powder with little cold milk.
2 Put rest of milk in saucepan with 1 tablespoon sugar.
3 When boiling pour over blancmange mixture, return to pan and cook until thick and smooth, stirring well.
4 Add 2 beaten egg yolks and 3 sliced bananas and cook for several minutes *without boiling*. Pour into warm dish.

5 Whisk eggs whites until stiff, fold in rest of sugar, pile in a circle on chocolate mixture.
6 Brown for 1 minute under grill then decorate with sliced banana, cherries, angelica.
7 Serve cold.

Baked bananas

Cooking time   15 minutes

You will need:

4–6 good-sized bananas	knob of butter
lemon juice	2 tablespoons brown sugar

1 Slice bananas into shallow dish.
2 Squeeze lemon juice over the fruit, dot with butter and a layer of sugar.
3 Bake for about 15 minutes in hot oven (425°F. —Gas Mark 6).
4 Serve with cream.

Banana and red currant whip

No cooking

You will need:

4 large bananas	squeeze of lemon juice
2 egg yolks	1 good tablespoon red
2 oz. sugar	currant jelly
$\frac{1}{2}$ pint whipped cream	

1 Beat egg yolks and sugar until creamy and fold in the cream.
2 Mash the bananas with the red currant jelly and lemon juice, fold into the cream.
3 Put into 4 shallow glasses and top with red currant jelly.

Banana slices

Cooking time   10 minutes

You will need:

4 large bananas	4 fingers sponge cake
little butter	brown sugar

1 Melt the butter in a pan and brown the sponge cakes in this.
2 Divide each banana in half and split each portion.
3 Heat in pan for a moment.
4 Put 4 pieces of banana on each of the 4 fingers, brush with hot butter from the pan, coat lavishly with brown sugar.
5 Put under a moderate grill to melt the sugar.
6 Serve at once.

Orange and banana fingers

As in preceding recipe, but add 1 or 2 oranges. Peel orange, cut into wafer-thin slices, put on to sponge fingers under the bananas.

Black currant crumble

Cooking time   30 minutes

You will need:

1 lb. black currants	little sugar and water

for the crumble

4 oz. flour (plain or self-raising)	2 oz. margarine
	3–4 oz. sugar

1 Put black currants into pie dish with little sugar and water.
2 Rub margarine into flour, add sugar.
3 Sprinkle over the fruit.
4 Bake for approximately 30 minutes in a moderately hot oven (400°F.—Gas Mark 5) until topping brown and fruit soft.

Caramel macaroni

Cooking time   12–15 minutes

You will need for 4–5 servings:

2 oz. quick cooking macaroni	2 level tablespoons cornflour
1 pint milk	whipped cream and toasted almonds for decoration (could be omitted)
2 bananas	
2 eating apples	
3 good tablespoons golden syrup	

1 Cook macaroni for 7 minutes in boiling salted water.
2 Drain.
3 Put syrup into strong saucepan and boil without stirring until a rich golden brown colour.
4 Blend cornflour with a little of the measured milk.
5 Add remaining milk to caramel.
6 Allow caramel to dissolve.
7 Add a little of the hot caramel milk to the blended cornflour.
8 Return to saucepan, boil 1 minute.
9 Add macaroni.
10 When cold cover with sliced bananas and grated fresh apple or sliced apple, top with whipped cream and chopped toasted almonds.

Cherry layer creams

Cooking time   10 minutes

You will need for 6–8 servings:

2 pints milk	1 teaspoon vanilla essence
1 oz. gelatine, softened in 2 tablespoons cold water	2 medium cans red cherries, stoned and halved
4 oz. fine semolina	2 egg yolks
4 oz. castor sugar	2 egg whites

1 Gently heat milk and gelatine in a large saucepan until gelatine dissolves.
2 Gradually add semolina and cook, stirring, until mixture comes to the boil and thickens.

3 Cook gently for another 3 minutes; remove from heat and stir in sugar and egg yolks.
4 Whisk egg whites until stiff and fold into semolina mixture.
5 Fill glass dessert dishes with alternate layers of halved cherries and semolina cream.
6 Garnish with cherry halves. Chill until lightly set.

Chocolate and pineapple cream

Cooking time   5 minutes

You will need:

1 packet chocolate blancmange powder	$\frac{3}{4}$ pint only of milk
pineapple and cream to decorate if wished	about 4 oz. chopped canned pineapple and little of the juice

1 Make the blancmange as directed on the packet, using only the $\frac{3}{4}$ pint milk.
2 Whisk in the pineapple and juice and put into glasses.
3 Top with pineapple and cream.
4 Serve hot or cold.

Coconut queen of puddings

Cooking time   approximately 1–1$\frac{1}{2}$ hours

You will need:

raspberry jam	angelica
2 oz. desiccated coconut plus 1 level tablespoon for meringue	1 pint milk
	2 large eggs
	3–4 oz. sugar
2 oz. breadcrumbs	cherries

1 Spread raspberry jam at bottom of a pie dish.
2 Beat egg yolks with 1–2 oz. sugar, add the crumbs and coconut.
3 Heat milk, pour over egg mixture and put into dish.
4 Bake for approximately 45 minutes in very moderate oven (350°F.—Gas Mark 3) until just firm.
5 Spread raspberry jam on top.
6 Whisk egg whites stiffly, fold in 2 oz. sugar and coconut. Do this very carefully to keep fluffy texture of meringue.
7 Pile on sweet.
8 Decorate with cherries and angelica.
9 Set for 15–25 minutes in very moderate oven until just golden brown.
10 Serve hot.

Coffee and marshmallow foam

Cooking time   few minutes
You will need:

8 oz. marshmallows
2 egg whites
1 good tablespoon
  chopped blanched
  almonds
¾ gill strong hot coffee
1 gill whipped evaporated

milk (or creamy
  custard or cream)
1 good tablespoon
  chopped glacé cherries
  or pineapple
1 dessertspoon crystallized
orange peel

1 Put the marshmallows, cut into halves, into
  a basin and stand this over a saucepan of hot
  water.
2 Pour the coffee over the marshmallows and
  leave until dissolved.
3 Allow the mixture to cool, but not become
  really stiff again.
4 Stir in the whipped cream, or evaporated milk
  or custard, the nuts, cherries and peel.
5 Lastly fold in the very stiffly beaten egg
  whites.
6 Pile into glasses and decorate with tiny pieces
  of cherry or pineapple.

Coffee pudding

Pressure cooking time   45 minutes
You will need:

2 oz. breadcrumbs
2 oz. margarine
few drops vanilla
  essence
4 oz. flour (2 teaspoons
  baking powder if
  using plain flour)

2 oz. sugar
1 egg
¼ pint strong coffee (just
  under)

1 Rub margarine into the flour, add baking
  powder, crumbs and sugar.
2 Mix with the coffee, egg and vanilla essence.
3 Put into a greased basin, stand basin on rack
  in cooker in 2 pints *boiling* water and cover
  well.
4 Fix the lid but do not put on pressure weight.
5 Steam rapidly for 15 minutes then put on
  pressure weight and bring to pressure of 5 lb.
6 Lower the heat and cook for 30 minutes.
7 Reduce pressure at once.
8 Serve with chocolate sauce or custard.

Duchess creams

Cooking time   5 minutes
You will need:

1 pint of sweetened
  custard (sauce
  consistency)
½ gill water
1 oz. sultanas

finely grated rind and
  juice of 2 oranges
½ oz. powdered gelatine
1 oz. crystallized orange
  peel
1 orange for decorating

1 Add grated rind to the custard while hot, then
  add gelatine dissolved in hot water.
2 Stir in the sultanas and crystallized peel and
  cool slightly, then add the orange juice. If this
  measures less than 1 gill add a little water.
3 Pour into sundae glasses and allow to set
  lightly.
4 Decorate with pieces of orange.

French pancakes

Cooking time   15 minutes
You will need:

2 oz. rice-flour or flour
2 oz. butter
2 oz. sugar
2 eggs

1½ gills milk
lemon rind
jam

1 Thoroughly grease 12 flat round tins (or
  saucers).
2 Cream the butter and sugar, beat in the yolks
  of the eggs with a little flour. Add the remainder
  of the flour with the milk and lemon juice.
3 Fold in the whites of the eggs, stiffly beaten,
  and pour into the tins.
4 Bake in a hot oven (450°F.—Gas Mark 7)
  until well risen, brown and firm—about 10
  minutes.
5 Turn on to a sugared paper, put a little hot
  jam on each and sandwich 2 rounds together.
6 Pile neatly on a hot dish and dust with castor
  sugar.

Fruit fritters

Cooking time   7–10 minutes
You will need:

to make the fritter batter
4 oz. self-raising flour
  (or plain flour with
  1 teaspoon baking
  powder)

1 oz. melted butter (or
  margarine or olive oil)
1 or 2 eggs
½ pint milk
1 oz. sugar

1 Sieve the dry ingredients together, add the egg
  (or eggs) and the milk.
2 Lastly add the melted butter. This is not
  essential but helps to give a crisp fritter.
3 For a very light fritter the egg yolks should
  be put in first, and when you have a very
  smooth thick batter fold in the stiffly beaten
  egg whites at the very end.
4 Coat the fruit and fry *steadily* in shallow fat
  or in deep fat if preferred. This makes sure
  that the outside is brown and the fruit hot
  or well cooked, whereas if the fritters are fried
  too quickly you get the outside browning
  before the middle is cooked.
5 Drain on kitchen or crumpled tissue paper and
  dredge well with sugar. Fill with one of the
  following:

Apples. Choose good cooking apples. Peel, core and cut into thin slices. coat with the batter. It is a good idea to flour the apples before coating in the batter to help it 'stick' well.

Pineapple. Well-drain rings of pineapple, then proceed as for apples.

Bananas. Halve if wished and add a little rum or rum essence to the batter.

mixed
Fruit fritters

Cooking time   10 minutes

You will need:

4 large slices of bread	little milk
butter for frying	2 oz. glacé cherries
2 oz. sultanas	2 oz. walnuts or blanched
2 or 3 tablespoons	almonds
apricot jam	little sugar
1 egg	

1 Cut the bread into attractive shapes.
2 Beat the egg and milk together.
3 Add a little sugar.
4 Dip the bread in this and fry in the butter until golden brown.
5 Meanwhile heat the apricot jam in a pan, add the sultanas, cherries and nuts and pile on the fritters.

Fruit cups

Cooking time   30 minutes

You will need:

1 lb. fruit (apples,	1½ oz. butter
plums etc)	water and sugar
3 oz. soft breadcrumbs	juice and grated rind of
2 tablespoons brown	2 oranges
sugar	

1 Simmer fruit with sugar, orange juice and very little water.
2 When fruit is just soft, but unbroken, put into fireproof dishes.
3 Toss crumbs in hot butter, add brown sugar and orange rind.
4 Sprinkle on top of each fruit cup and bake for 20 minutes in a moderately hot oven (400 °F. – Gas Mark 5).

Fruit pudding

Pressure cooking time   1 hour

You will need:

8 oz. suet crust pastry	2 pints water
1–1½ lb. fruit*	sugar
	water

* This can be varied according to the season, apples, and blackberries, rhubarb, blackcurrants, etc. If using apples half fill the dish with water.

1 Line a well-greased basin with part of the suet crust.
2 Put the fruit into the pastry with a good sprinkling of sugar and a little water.
3 Roll out the rest of the dough to form a cover.
4 Damp edges of the pastry lid and press on to the pudding.
5 Cover well.
6 Stand on rack in cooker in 2 pints BOILING water.
7 Fix the lid but do NOT put on pressure weight.
8 Steam for 20 minutes.
9 Bring to 5 lb. pressure, lower the heat and cook for 40 minutes.
10 Reduce pressure.
11 Serve with a custard sauce.

Frosted chocolate pudding

Cooking time   25 minutes

You will need:

1 pint milk	4 oz. grated chocolate or
3 eggs	2 oz. chocolate powder
1 oz. cornflour	5 oz. sugar

1 Blend cornflour with a little cold milk.
2 Bring rest of milk, with grated chocolate, to the boil.
3 Add to cornflour and return to heat with 2 oz. of the sugar and cook until thick.
4 Cool slightly add egg yolks and complete cooking WITHOUT boiling for 10 minutes.
5 Pour into dish.
6 Whip egg whites, fold in last of the sugar.
7 Pile on chocolate mixture and set in a moderate oven (375°F.—Gas Mark 4) for 10 minutes.
8 Serve at once.

Orange chocolate pudding

Cooking time   25 minutes

1 Recipe as above, but add finely grated rind of 2 oranges to the cornflour mixture.
2 Skin the oranges and cut into wafer thin slices: arrange on top of the cornflour mixture, before putting on the meringue.
3 Set as before. This combination of orange and chocolate is delicious.

10 ways to dress up fresh fruit

Apples can be grated and added to lightly whipped cream or beaten into ice-cream. Top with grated chocolate.

Bananas can be fried in a little butter or baked in the oven (baked bananas, page 66), but they are also extremely good mashed with lemon juice and beaten into ice-cream. There are a number of quick banana recipes (see pages 66, 77, 88).

Blackcurrants can be added to jellies raw or they make a very good fresh blackcurrant fool by mashing and beating into ice-cream.

Grapefruit can be served as a sweet if the sections are mixed with a little sherry and sugar and piled on ice-cream.

Melon as well as being an excellent hors-d'oeuvre is a first class sweet. Divide into portions and mix the fruit with mandarin oranges or fresh oranges. Top with cream.

Oranges can be baked with sugar and butter (see page 67) but they make an excellent fruit compote. Peel the oranges, cut into rings and arrange them in a shallow dish. Sprinkle with sugar and add sherry or kirsch. Leave for several hours. Serve with cream or ice-cream.

Pears can be halved and coated with hot red currant jelly. When heating the jelly dilute with a little water. Or cover them with melted chocolate and serve with cream or ice-cream. When melting the chocolate do this in a basin over hot water, add just a little water.

Raspberries have such a delicious flavour that most people prefer them with sugar and cream. But if you want to make a very quick sweet, mash them to a pulp, and pile on rounds of sponge cake. Allow the raspberries to soak into the sponge a little, then top with whipped cream.

Red currants are an excellent dessert fruit. Arrange sprigs of these in a shallow dish and sprinkle with sugar so they become slightly frosted or crush the red currants with sugar and a few drops of vanilla essence or with vanilla sugar if this is obtainable in your store. Serve with yoghourt, cream or ice-cream.

Strawberries make an excellent filling for pancakes or can be served in salads with cream cheese. They also produce a delicious fruit salad, if halved and mixed with sliced banana.

Gooseberry and lemon jelly

Cooking time   15 minutes

You will need:

12 oz. green gooseberries	cream to decorate
sugar to taste	½ pint water
	1 lemon-flavoured jelly

1 Make a syrup of the sugar and water and put in the gooseberries when the sugar has completely dissolved.
2 Simmer until the fruit is soft, lift out a few gooseberries for decoration and continue cooking the remainder until a pulp.
3 Rub through a sieve and measure the pulp and syrup.
4 Add enough water to give nearly 1¼ pints altogether.
5 Dissolve the lemon jelly in this hot mixture and put into a mould.
Turn out and decorate with cream and the whole fruit.

Grapefruit oat brûlée

Cooking time   few minutes

You will need:

	2 tablespoons rolled oats
2 grapefruits	2 tablespoons golden
1 oz. butter	syrup

1 Halve and prepare grapefruit.
2 Melt butter in saucepan.
3 Add oats and syrup.
4 Mix thoroughly.
5 Divide oat mixture into 4.

6 Sprinkle over grapefruit.

7 Place under medium hot electric grill until lightly browned and crisp on top.

Hawaiian pie

Cooking time   10 minutes

You will need:

2 oz. butter or margarine (preferably unsalted)
2 oz. castor sugar

1 dessertspoon golden syrup
4 oz. crushed cornflakes

for filling

1 can pineapple rings
glacé cherries
whipped cream (if available)

2 tablespoons pineapple jam (apricot jam can be used)

1 Cream butter, sugar and syrup together, then work in cornflakes.

2 Form into flan shape.

3 Open can of pineapple rings and arrange fruit in flan case.

4 Blend 2 tablespoons pineapple syrup from can with pineapple jam, spread over fruit.

5 Decorate with glacé cherries and whipped cream.

6 Allow flan to harden before serving.

Ice-cream medley

Ice-cream is a sure favourite and enables you to give the family a popular sweet with little or no trouble. Here are some quick ideas.

1 Melt fudge in a double saucepan and pour over the ice-cream.

2 Beat well-drained chopped pineapple into the ice-cream and chopped walnuts to taste.

3 Add grated dessert apples to the ice-cream and put into glasses. Decorate with crystallized ginger.

4 Top ice-cream with cherry brandy and cream.

Jelly omelette

Cooking time   5–8 minutes

You will need:

3 large eggs
1 oz. butter
1 oz. sugar
½ teaspoon vanilla

essence or cherry brandy
hot jam or jelly
icing sugar or castor sugar

1 Separate the eggs.

2 Whisk the egg yolks and sugar together.

3 Add the essence, then fold in the stiffly beaten egg whites.

4 Heat the butter in an omelette pan and pour in the egg mixture.

5 Cook steadily until set on the bottom then put under a medium grill to cook the top.

6 Fill with the jam or jelly.

7 Fold and serve at once, dusted with icing sugar or castor sugar.

Kissel

Cooking time   15 minutes

You will need:

1 lb. soft fruit
1 tablespoon cornflour
1 gill water

3 tablespoons golden syrup or honey

1 This delicious sweet is very simple to make. Put the fruit with water and syrup or honey into a pan.

2 Simmer until soft, then beat or sieve.

3 Stir on to cornflour and return to pan, cooking until smooth and clear.

4 Allow to cool.

5 Decorate with cream if possible.

Lemon and apricot mousse

No cooking time, just a few minutes to dissolve the jelly

You will need:

1 lemon-flavoured jelly
3 egg whites
1 medium-sized can apricots

¾ pint lightly whipped cream or evaporated milk

1 Open can of apricots and pour out the juice. Add enough water to give ¼ pint liquid.

2 Heat this and dissolve in it the lemon jelly.

3 When cold, add cream and stiffly beaten egg whites.

4 Put most of the apricots at the bottom of a shallow dish.

5 Pile the mixture on top.

6 When firm, decorate with the remaining apricots.

Lemon and coconut jelly

Cooking time   few minutes

You will need:

juice of 2 lemons
½ pint water
little cream and sections of orange to decorate
2–3 oz. desiccated coconut

2–3 oz. sugar
1 tablespoon powdered gelatine
2 egg whites (the yolks can be used in almond cream, see page 65)

1 Soften the gelatine in the lemon juice, then pour on the very hot water, adding the sugar.

2 Allow to cool.

3 When just beginning to thicken, stir in coconut and stifly beaten egg whites.

4 Pour into a mould and when set turn out and decorate with whipped cream or fresh orange.

Lemon and coconut mould

Cooking time   few minutes

You will need:

1 lemon jelly	2 oz. sponge cake crumbs
2 oz. desiccated coconut	2 eggs
few pieces glacé cherry	1–2 oz. sugar
and blanched almonds	

1 Dissolve jelly in just over $\frac{3}{4}$ pint boiling water.
2 Beat egg yolks and sugar until light.
3 Add coconut, crumbs and the lemon jelly.
4 Leave to set lightly, then fold in stiffly beaten egg whites.
5 Pour into mould and when quite firm, unmould and decorate with cherry and nuts.

Macaroon cream

Cooking time   few minutes for custard

You will need:

$\frac{3}{4}$ pint sweetened custard	1 dessertspoon powder gelatine
1 gill water	few drops almond essence
2 oz. blanched almonds	3 average-sized
few glacé cherries	macaroons, crumbled

1 Dissolve gelatine in water, then add to hot custard, almond essence and crumbs.
2 Pour into mould and leave to set.
3 Split almonds and brown in oven or under the grill.
4 Turn out cream and decorate with almonds and cherries.

Melba sauce

Cooking time   10 minutes

You will need:

5 oz. raspberries*	1 tablespoon sugar
2–3 oz. red currant or	1 teaspoon cornflour
apple jelly	2 tablespoons water
* fresh, frozen or canned – omit sugar with latter	

1 Blend cornflour with water.
2 Put all ingredients into pan and cook gently until thickened.
3 Rub through a sieve if desired.

Economical
Melba sauce

Cooking time   10 minutes

You will need:

2–3 oz. raspberry jam	$\frac{1}{2}$ gill water
2–3 oz. red currant jelly	$\frac{1}{2}$ teaspoon arrowroot or cornflour

1 Blend the arrowroot or cornflour with the water.
2 Put into a saucepan with the other ingredients.
3 Cook until clear and slightly thickened.
4 Cool before using.

Mincemeat shortcakes

Cooking time   13 minutes

You will need:

8 oz. flour (with plain flour use 2 level teaspoons baking powder)	mincemeat
	2 oz. butter or margarine or vegetable shortening
	3 oz. sugar
1 egg	milk to mix

1 Sieve flour, rub in fat and add sugar, egg and enough milk to make a sticky dough.
2 Put spoonfuls of mixture on greased tin and bake for 10 minutes in really hot oven (450–475 °F. Gas Mark 7–8).
3 Top with mincemeat, re-heat for 2–3 minutes and serve at once.
4 Instead of mincemeat thick fruit purée can be used.

Mixed fruit Bavarian cream

Cooking time   8–10 minutes

You will need:

1 vanilla flavoured blancmange powder	2 oz. chopped glacé cherries
1 pint milk	1 oz. chopped almonds
$\frac{1}{4}$ pint whipped cream or evaporated milk	1 oz. chopped glacé pineapple (if wished)
2 oz. sugar	2 oz. sultanas

1 Make blancmange in usual way, adding sugar and most of the fruit mixture.
2 Allow to cool, stirring well to prevent skin forming.
3 Fold in cream.
4 Pour into rinsed mould and allow to set.
5 Turn out and decorate with more cream and pieces of fruit.

Mocha meringue

Cooking time   10–15 minutes

You will need:

1 packet chocolate-flavoured blancmange powder	small piece of chocolate
	$\frac{1}{2}$ pint milk
	$\frac{1}{2}$ pint strong coffee
2 eggs	4 oz. sugar

1 Make the blancmange as directed on the packet, using milk and coffee instead of all milk.
2 Add 2 oz. sugar and the egg yolks and cook gently for a few minutes, without boiling.
3 Put into a dish.
4 Fold the rest of the sugar into the stiffly beaten egg whites, pile over the sweet and brown either in the oven or under a hot grill.
5 Decorate with grated chocolate.

Mocha walnut pudding

Cooking time   30 minutes

You will need:

1 chocolate flavoured blancmange powder	$\frac{3}{4}$ pint milk
2 oz. chopped walnuts	$\frac{1}{4}$ pint strong coffee
2 eggs yolks	1 oz. sugar
	2 oz. fine breadcrumbs

for meringue

2 egg whites	2 oz. sugar
	few halved walnuts

1 Blend the blancmange powder with a little cold milk, bring rest of milk to the boil, pour over the blended blancmange powder, return to pan with sugar and coffee.
2 Cook until thickened.
3 Stir in the nuts and crumbs, then the beaten egg yolks.
4 Put into a pie dish.
5 Whip egg whites until very stiff, fold in the sugar, pile over coffee and chocolate mixture, decorate with halved walnuts and set for about 20 minutes in a slow oven (300°F.—Gas Mark 2).

Orange and banana salad

Cooking time   5 minutes

You will need:

2 bananas, sliced	juice and rind of 1 orange
$\frac{1}{2}$ gill water	2 oranges, sliced
1 tablespoon sugar	

1 Boil water, sugar and grated orange rind for 5 minutes.
2 Strain, add orange juice.
3 Peel and slice the remaining oranges and bananas, pour over the syrup.

Orange surprise

Cooking time   3 minutes

You will need:

4 oranges (or 2 very large ones)	little ice-cream
2 oz. castor sugar	2 egg whites

1 Cut tops off oranges and scoop out centre. Chop.
2 Put back into orange cases with ice-cream and a little sugar.
3 Whisk egg whites, fold in sugar.
4 Pile on top of ice-cream and oranges and brown for 3 minutes in a very hot oven (475°F. —Gas Mark 8).

Orange surprises

Cooking time   30 minutes

You will need:

4 good-sized oranges	2 level tablespoons cornflour or custard powder
2 eggs	
3 oz. sugar	small pieces angelica

1 Cut the oranges into halves, squeeze out the juice very gently without breaking the cases, remove pith and pips:
2 Measure juice, add enough water to give $\frac{3}{4}$ pint liquid.
3 Blend the cornflour or custard powder with this, put into pan with 1 oz. sugar and thicken.
4 Remove from heat and cool slightly.
5 Add egg yolks, then thicken gently without boiling.
6 Make sure the 8 orange halves are standing firmly and fill them with mixture.
7 Whisk egg whites until stiff, fold in the rest of the sugar, pile on top of orange mixture and return to very moderate oven for approximately 20 minutes.
8 Decorate with leaves of angelica.

Pancake batter

You will need:

4 oz. flour	1 egg
pinch salt	$\frac{1}{2}$ pint milk or milk and water

rich pancake batter

4 oz. flour	2 eggs
pinch salt	just under $\frac{1}{2}$ pint milk or milk and water
1 tablespoon olive oil	

1 Sieve flour and salt, add egg or eggs and enough milk to give sticky consistency.
2 Beat well then gradually add rest of liquid.
3 Add oil last if using this.

Hot peach Condé

Cooking time   35 minutes—$1\frac{1}{4}$ hours

You will need:

2 oz. rice or large can creamed rice	$\frac{1}{4}$ pint juice from canned peaches
1 pint milk	1 teaspoon cornflour
little vanilla essence or vanilla pod	2 egg whites
	3 oz. sugar
	sliced peaches

1 Cook the rice with the milk, 1 oz. sugar, vanilla flavouring, until just tender and soft. Remove vanilla pod.
2 Pour into hot dish.
3 If using canned rice pour into hot dish from can.
4 Whisk egg whites stiffly, fold in sugar, pile or pipe round edge of dish. Put into cool oven (275–300°F.—Gas Mark 1–2) for about 30–45 minutes until meringue is firm and golden brown.
5 Meanwhile thicken syrup with the cornflour, cooking until thick and clear.
6 Pile sliced peaches in centre of dish and cover with hot thickened syrup.
7 Serve at once.

Flapjack peach crumble

Cooking time   35 minutes

You will need:

3 oz. butter
1 oz. castor sugar
2 tablespoons golden syrup
6 oz. rolled oats
¼ teaspoon salt
1 medium-sized can of sliced peaches
1 oz. chopped blanched almonds

1 Cream butter and sugar until light and fluffy.
2 Add syrup, and cream a few minutes longer.
3 Gradually work in oats and salt until mixture is well blended.
4 Place drained sliced peaches and almonds in greased pie dish.
5 Spread flapjack mixture on top.
6 Bake on the middle shelf of a moderate oven (375°F.—Gas Mark 4) for 35 minutes.

Quick chocolate mousse

Cooking time   5 minutes

You will need for 2 servings:

4 oz. chocolate (preferably plain chocolate)
2 dessertspoons cream
2 eggs
2 dessertspoons sugar

1 Grate chocolate.
2 Put sugar, chocolate and egg yolk in a basin over hot water and beat together until smooth.
3 Cool slightly.
4 Add cream and when quite cold fold in stiffly beaten egg whites.
5 Pour into 2 small glasses and serve with biscuits.

Quick fruit dumplings

Cooking time   10–15 minutes

You will need:

4 oz. self-raising flour
½ oz. sugar
4 tablespoons milk
pinch salt
2 oz. finely chopped suet
large can peach slices or halves or apricots or plums or rhubarb

1 Sift flour and salt into a bowl and add suet and sugar.
2 Mix to a fairly stiff consistency with the milk, then, with floured hands, shape into 8 dumplings.
3 Drain fruit and pour syrup into a large, shallow pan.
4 Bring to boil then put in dumplings.
5 Reduce heat, cover pan and poach slowly for 10–15 minutes.

6 Transfer dumplings to a warm serving dish, coat with syrup and decorate with warmed canned fruit.
7 If you do not wish to open a can of fruit try poaching the dumplings in a mixture of water and lemon juice sweetened to taste. Dust them with sugar before serving.

Caramel pears

Cooking time   20 minutes

You will need:

4 good-sized, firm, but not too hard pears
6 or 8 almonds
3 oz. sugar
1½ gills water

1 Put 3 tablespoons of the water and the sugar into a pan, stir until the sugar has dissolved then boil until dark brown.
2 Add the rest of the water and bring to the boil.
3 Peel, core and slice pears, put them into caramel, and cook for about 10 minutes.
4 Serve in glasses topped with blanched shredded almonds.

Quick pineapple mousse

Cooking time   few minutes

You will need:

½ can chopped pineapple*
1 dessertspoon powdered gelatine
cherries and angelica to decorate
2 eggs
1–2 dessertspoons castor sugar
3 dessertspoons water

*Pieces, cubes or slices can be used, in which case chop finely.

1 Dissolve the gelatine in the very hot water.
2 Put the pineapple, juice from can, sugar and egg yolks in a basin over hot water, beat together for about 5–10 minutes until creamy.
3 Leave to cool.
4 Add dissolved gelatine, then fold in stiffly beaten egg whites.
5 Put into fruit glasses and decorate with cherries and angelica.
6 Serve with biscuits or sponge cakes.

Raspberry mousse

Cooking time   few minutes

You will need:

1 small can raspberries or 6 oz. fresh fruit
1½ gills milk
1 raspberry-flavoured jelly
¼ pint evaporated milk
2 egg whites

1 Drain the fruit and measure the juice.
2 If necessary add enough water to give ¼ pint.
3 Dissolve the jelly in this thoroughly and when cool add the cold milk and the whipped evap-

orated milk, lastly fold in the stiffly beaten egg whites.

4 Pour into a rinsed mould and when firm turn out and decorate with the raspberries if wished.

Raspberry soufflé

Cooking time   12 minutes

You will need:

3 egg whites
2 tablespoons sugar
1 can raspberries or packet defrosted

raspberries (or use fresh raspberries and extra sugar)

1 Strain off juice from canned or frozen raspberries and mash the fruit.
2 Beat egg whites until very stiff, fold in the sugar and fruit.
3 Pour into buttered soufflé dish and bake for 12 minutes only in centre of moderately hot oven (400 °F. – Gas Mark 5).
4 Serve at once with the hot juice.

Rice creams

Cooking time   45 minutes

You will need:

3 oz. rice
1 pint milk
few tablespoons whipped cream

1 or 2 oz. sugar
little vanilla essence or grated orange or lemon rind to flavour

to decorate

jam or jelly   lightly whipped cream

1 Cook the rice with the milk, sugar and flavouring in the usual way until soft and tender.
2 Cool, then stir in the cream.
3 Put jam or jelly into 4 cups or small moulds and cover with rice.
4 Leave until quite cold and set, then turn out and top with whipped cream.
5 If preferred the jam can be warmed slightly with a little water to give a softer mixture and put over the rice moulds when turned out.

Strawberry croûtes

No cooking

You will need:

2 oblong sponge cakes
8 oz. fresh strawberries

little sugar
red currant jelly
cream

1 Cut sponge cakes through centre.
2 Put each half on small dish.
3 Spread liberally with red currant jelly.
4 Top with whipped cream and sweetened strawberries.

Strawberry Napoleons

Cooking time   8 minutes

You will need:

4 small square sponge cakes
4 large egg whites

8 oz. strawberries
6 tablespoons sugar

1 Crush most of the fruit, add a little of the sugar.
2 Spread over the 4 sponge cakes.
3 Whisk egg whites, fold in the rest of the sugar.
4 Pile over strawberry cakes, set for 5–8 minutes in a moderately hot oven (400 °F. – Gas Mark 5).
5 Decorate with rest of fruit.
6 Serve at once.

Strawberry-topped castle puddings

Cooking time   25–30 minutes

You will need:

4 oz. self-raising flour
4 oz. butter or margarine
2 eggs

strawberry jam
large pinch of salt
4 oz. castor sugar
few drops vanilla essence

1 Sift flour and salt together.
2 Cream fat, sugar and vanilla essence together until light and fluffy
3 Add eggs, 1 at a time, 1 tablespoon of the flour.
4 Fold in remaining flour.
5 Well-grease 6–9 individual pudding moulds (according to size) and $\frac{2}{3}$ fill with the mixture.
6 Cover each with greased paper or aluminium foil and steam for 25–30 minutes.
7 Turn out and top each pudding with a spoonful of strawberry jam.

Surprise pudding

Cooking time   10 minutes

You will need:
1 sponge cake
1 pint custard

1 lb. mixed summer fruit – black and red currants, raspberries, etc.

to decorate

whole fruit or glacé cherries

1 Cut a large circle from the middle of the sponge cake, leaving just a ring.
2 Stand on a serving dish.
3 Fill centre with the fruit and place part of the circle of sponge on top, making the cake look whole again.
4 Pour over the hot custard
5 Decorate with the fruit.
6 Serve hot or cold.

Sweet omelettes

Cooking time   10 minutes

You will need:

4 eggs	2 tablespoons cream
2 oz. sugar	from top of milk
1 oz. butter	jam or other flavourings

1 Separate the yolks from whites of the egg either by breaking the eggs carefully and tipping the white into a basin while retaining the yolk in the shell, or by breaking the whole egg on to a saucer, putting an egg-cup over the yolk and pouring the white into a basin.
2 Beat the yolks with the sugar and cream, then fold in stiffly beaten egg whites.
3 Heat the butter in the pan and pour in the egg mixture.
4 Cook steadily for several minutes until firm at the bottom.
5 Put under a medium grill or into the oven until the top is golden brown.
6 Fill with the hot jam and fold.
7 Top with more jam or sieved icing sugar and serve at once.

Suggestions for fillings

1 **Ginger marmalade omelette:** Fill with ginger marmalade and serve with cream.

2 **Almond macaroon omelette:** Add a crumbled macaroon biscuit, few drops of almond essence to the yolks and fill and top with warm apricot jam and chopped almonds.

3 **Apricot omelette:** Fill with canned apricots and serve with hot apricot syrup.

4 **Ice-cream omelette:** Fill with ice-cream and serve with hot chocolate sauce.

5 **Glazed omelette:** Fill with apple purée or other thick fruit purée, top with quite a thick layer of sieved icing sugar and put under the grill to brown. Watch it most carefully.

6 **Orange omelette:** Add grated orange rind and orange juice instead of cream to the egg yolks. Fill with sliced oranges.

Uncooked flan

No cooking

Yeu will need:

2 oz. margarine or	cream or ice-cream
butter	2 oz. sugar
1 good teaspoon	approximately 4 oz.
golden syrup	cornflakes
	sliced fruit

1 To make flan, cream margarine, sugar and syrup.

2 Crush cornflakes slightly with a rolling pin.
3 Work into margarine mixture until firm texture.
4 Press into flan shape on plate.
5 Leave until ready to serve, then fill with sliced fruit and top with cream or ice-cream.

Vanilla soufflés

Cooking time   25 minutes

You will need:

1 packet vanilla-flavoured blancmange or $1\frac{1}{2}$ oz. cornflour and a few drops vanilla essence (or vanilla pod)	2 tablespoons cream or evaporated milk
	1 pint milk
	2 oz. castor sugar
	3 eggs
	icing sugar

1 If using vanilla pod, put this into pan with the milk. Heat together.
2 Remove pod. Blend cornflour or blancmange powder with a little cold milk.
3 Bring rest of milk to the boil (add vanilla essence now, if using this), pour over cornflour, return to the pan with sugar and bring to the boil, stirring all the time until thick and smooth.
4 Remove from heat, add egg yolks beaten with cream and, lastly, stiffly beaten egg whites.
5 Put into 4 ovenproof dishes and bake for approximately 20 minutes in a moderate oven (375 °F. – Gas Mark 4).
6 Dust with sieved icing sugar and serve at once.

Chocolate soufflé
Use either chocolate-flavoured blancmange or 1 oz. cornflour and 1 dessertspoon cocoa.

Rum soufflé
Omit vanilla flavouring, add 1 or 2 tablespoons rum or a little rum essence.

Coffee soufflé
Use $\frac{1}{4}$ pint strong coffee and $\frac{3}{4}$ pint milk.

To whip evaporated milk

To whip evaporated milk with the greatest efficiency, boil the can of milk for about 15 minutes in a pan of water, then thoroughly chill for several hours. Turn into a large bowl and whisk firmly.

For very thick cream from evaporated milk, turn the milk out of the can after the 15 minutes boiling (open the can carefully so the milk does not spurt out) and stir on to a teaspoon powdered gelatine, dissolved in 2 tablespoons very hot water. Cool as before, then whip.

To save time it is a good idea to boil several cans of evaporated milk at one time and store them in a cool place. They are then ready to whisk.

Some people omit the gelatine and add a little lemon juice to the evaporated milk instead.

Yoghourt and oat special

No cooking time

You will need for 3–4 servings:

2 bottles plain yoghourt	4 rounded tablespoons rolled oats

2 level dessertspoons golden syrup	2 oz. seedless raisins
2 oz. walnuts (roughly chopped)	2 level dessertspoons castor sugar
glacé cherries for decoration	2 eating apples (finely chopped)

1 Put yoghourt into mixing bowl.
2 Add rolled oats, raisins, castor sugar, syrup, apples and walnuts.
3 Mix thoroughly.
4 Leave a few hours.
5 Serve topped with glacé cherries.

Chapter 8

Cakes and Biscuits

Many people feel when they are short of time they cannot produce home-made cakes, but do remember that modern cake mixes can be used as a basis for your home-made cakes and you can decorate them in any way you wish.

This saves you a great deal of time by cutting out preliminary preparations.

Another way in which time can be saved is to make up a batch of mixture and use it in several ways. As an example of this see cake mixtures 1 and 2, pages 78–9.

Almond cookies

Cooking time   12–15 minutes

You will need:

6 oz. flour	egg yolks to mix
3 oz. ground almonds	egg white to brush top
6 oz. sugar	little sugar
3 oz. margarine	

1 Cream margarine and sugar until soft and light.
2 Add ground almonds, flour and enough egg yolk to bind.
3 Roll out to about $\frac{1}{3}$ inch thick, cut into squares, then make several slits in the dough.
4 Brush with egg white and little sugar.
5 Bake for 12–15 minutes in a moderate oven (375°F.—Gas Mark 4).

Almond shorties

Cooking time   15 minutes

You will need:

3 oz. butter	$\frac{1}{2}$ oz. cornflour
2 oz. sugar	1 oz. ground almonds
3 oz. flour	

1 Rub butter into sieved flour and cornflour.
2 Work in sugar and ground almonds.
3 Roll out thinly on a floured board.
4 Cut into rounds and bake for 12–15 minutes in centre of moderate oven (375°F.—Gas Mark 4).
5 When cold, coat with almond-flavoured icing if wished and pipe lines of coffee icing.

Banana and rum pastries

Cooking time   15 minutes

You will need:

6 oz. short crust or sweet short crust pastry (see page 86)	glacé cherries
	little red currant jelly
	$\frac{1}{4}$ pint whipped cream
3 bananas	2 teaspoons rum
3 teaspoons sugar	icing sugar

1 Line 12 patty tins with the pastry.
2 Bake until crisp and brown in hot oven.
3 Spread with a little red currant jelly.
4 Mash bananas with rum and sugar.
5 Fold in whipped cream.
6 Fill tarts with this mixture, dust tops liberally with sieved icing sugar and decorate with glacé cherries.

Basic cake mixture number 1

This is 'rubbed in' mixture, and can be used for sweet pastry, biscuits, puddings and cakes. It is a wonderful standby as it can be used in so many different ways, and there is no need to use it all up on the day that it is made. It can be stored in a jar or plastic bag until required.

You will need:

1 lb. flour (with plain flour use 2 level teaspoons baking powder)	8 oz. margarine
	4 oz. castor sugar

1 Sieve flour.
2 Rub in margarine.
3 Add sugar.

variations:

Jam or fruit fingers

Cooking time   approximately 20 minutes

You will need:

¼ basic cake mixture	jam, or jelly with chopped
1 egg (optional)	fresh fruit, or canned
a little water	fruit with glaze made by
cream	boiling 1 teaspoon
	cornflour or arrowroot
	with 1 gill fruit syrup

1 Add water, or egg and water to mixture, until of right consistency to roll.
2 Roll out and form into long oblong.
3 Flute the edges, prick, and bake 'blind' in a hot oven for about 20 minutes (450°F.—Gas Mark 7).
4 When crisp and golden brown, spread with jam and top with cream.
5 Or top with set jelly, to which is added chopped fresh fruit.
6 Or top with canned fruit, and cover with a glaze made by boiling the cornflour or arrowroot with the fruit syrup.
7 Decorate with whipped cream and cut into fingers.

Chocolate honey buns

Cooking time   approximately 12 minutes
You will need:

¼ basic cake mixture	bar of plain or milk
1 tablespoon honey	chocolate (chopped)
1 egg	

1 Combine honey and egg with mixture.
2 Add chopped chocolate and mix thoroughly.
3 Put in little heaps on well greased baking tins, allowing room for the cakes to spread slightly.
4 Bake in a hot oven (450°F.—Gas Mark 7) for about 12 minutes.

Lemon and orange biscuits

Cooking time   approximately 10 minutes
You will need:

¼ basic cake mixture	lemon and orange juice
grated rind of 1	to bind
lemon and 1 orange	curd or icing for filling

1 Add sugar and grated fruit rind to basic mixture.
2 Add sufficient fruit juice to give proper rolling consistency.
3 Roll out as thinly as possible. The thinner the dough, the crisper the biscuits will be.
4 Cut into any desired shapes, or if in a hurry, into fingers.
5 If ¼ inch thick, bake for about 10 minutes in a moderate oven (375°F.—Gas Mark 4–5).
6 Cool on baking tin.

Apple or mixed fruit pudding

Cooking time   40 minutes
You will need:

¼ basic cake mixture	1 oz. desiccated
1 oz. brown sugar	coconut
¼ teaspoon mixed	apples or other fruit
spice	little water or sugar

1 Combine brown sugar, spice, coconut with basic mixture.
2 Put sliced apples or other fruit into a dish, adding a little water and sugar.
3 Cover with topping and cook in the centre of a very moderate oven (375°F.—Gas Mark 4) for approximately 40 minutes.

Basic cake mixture number 2

This is a creamed mixture, for lighter cakes, puddings, etc.

You will need:

12 oz. margarine	1 lb. flour (with plain
12 oz. sugar	flour, use 4 level
6 eggs	teaspoons baking
	powder)

1 Cream the margarine and sugar until soft and light.
2 Beat the eggs, and add gradually to the creamed mixture.
3 Sieve the flour and baking powder.
4 Stir gently into the egg and margarine mixture, taking care not to over-beat.

For greater economy use only 4 eggs and 4 tablespoons milk.

variations:

Coconut fruit loaf

Cooking time   approximately 1 hour

You will need:

¼ basic cake mixture	6 oz. dried fruit
for topping	
1 oz. brown sugar	1 oz coconut
1 oz. margarine	1 oz. walnuts

1 Add fruit to basic mixture. No extra liquid is required.
2 Put into loaf tin.
3 Make topping by creaming sugar with margarine, adding coconut and finely chopped walnuts.
4 Spread on top of loaf.
5 Bake for about 1 hour in the centre of a moderate oven (375 °F. – Gas Mark 4). This delicious loaf is excellent for carrying on a picnic.

Madeleines

Cooking time   approximately 10 minutes

You will need:

¼ basic mixture	cherries
jam or curd	OR whipped cream and
coconut	few drops Tia Maria

1 Half fill dariole moulds (castle pudding tins) with the basic mixture.
2 Bake for about 10 minutes in a hot oven (425–450 °F. – Gas Mark 6–7).

3 Turn out and when cold coat with jam or curd and roll in coconut. Top with a cherry.
4 For luxury Madeleines coat with whipped cream flavoured with a few drops Tia Maria and then roll in grated coconut. Top with whipped cream.

Ice-cream cake

Cooking time   approximately 20 minutes

You will need:

¼ basic mixture	fruit
1 tablespoon milk	whipped cream
ice-cream	

1 Add milk to basic mixture.
2 Bake in a fairly good sized square sandwich tin, or 9-inch round tin for about 20 minutes in a moderate oven (375–400 °F.—Gas Mark 6–7).
3 Turn out and top with scoops of ice-cream, fruit and whipped cream. This makes a wonderful dessert.

Crisp shortbread cookies

Cooking time   approximately 12–15 minutes

You will need:

	1 oz. cornflour
¼ basic mixture	(flavoured
glacé cherries	if desired)

1 Add cornflour to basic mixture.
2 Roll into balls and top each with a piece of cherry.
3 Bake for approximately 12–15 minutes in a moderate oven (375°F.—Gas Mark 4). This mixture makes very crisp shortbread-like cookies.

Cheese cake

Cooking time   55 minutes

You will need:

	6 oz. rich short crust pastry (see page 86)
for the filling	
1 LEVEL tablespoon flour	8 oz. cream or cottage cheese
seasoning	2 eggs or 3 if rather small
2 oz. sugar	
1–2 oz. butter	2 oz. sultanas

1 Line a 7-inch flan ring with thin pastry, keep a little over.
2 Set 'blind' for about 10 minutes in a hot oven.
3 Cream butter and cheese and add all other ingredients gradually.
4 Put into pastry case.
5 Put a lattice work of very thin pastry on top and bake for about 45 minutes in the centre of a moderate oven (375 °F. – Gas Mark 4) until filling is brown and firm.

Cheese and almond cookies

Cooking time   15 minutes

You will need:

2½ oz. margarine	seasoning
1½ oz. grated cheese	egg white
1 oz. chopped almonds	1 tablespoon grated cheese
blanched almonds	
4 oz. flour (with plain flour use 1 level teaspoon baking powder)	

1 Cream margarine, 1½ oz. cheese and seasoning.
2 Add chopped almonds and flour.
3 Roll into balls, put on lightly greased tins, allowing room to flatten.
4 Brush with egg white, sprinkle cheese on top, arrange almonds in a pattern, bake for 12–15 minutes in centre of moderate oven (375 °F. – Gas Mark 4).
5 Cool on tin.

Chestnut tart

Cooking time 25 minutes

You will need:

4 oz. short crust pastry (see page 86)
can chestnut purée
2–3 oz. chocolate
whipped cream
2 oz. margarine
3 oz. sieved icing sugar
½ teaspoon vanilla essence

1 Line a flan tin with pastry and bake until crisp and brown in hot oven. (425–450 °F. – Gas Mark 6–7).
2 Mix chestnut purée with creamed margarine and sugar.
3 Add vanilla.
4 Spread over the bottom of the flan.
5 Melt chocolate with a FEW DROPS only of water.
6 Pour on top of the chestnut purée when cold.
7 Decorate with rosettes of whipped cream.

Chinese 'chews'

Cooking time 25–35 minutes

You will need:

2 oz. margarine
2 oz. brown sugar
4 oz. self-raising flour
2 oz. chopped glacé cherries
icing sugar
1 dessertspoon syrup or treacle
1 egg
4 oz. chopped dates
2 oz. chopped walnuts
2 oz. chopped peel
grated lemon rind

1 Sieve flour, rub in the margarine.
2 Add all the other ingredients.
3 Grease and flour a square shallow tin, measuring 7 or 8 inches across.
4 Put in the cake mixture at 400 °F. – Gas Mark 5 for about 25–35 minutes.
5 Remove from tin.
6 Cut into fingers and dredge with icing sugar.

Chocolate almond tarts

Cooking time 20 minutes

You will need:

4 oz. sweet short crust pastry (see page 86)
2 egg whites
3 oz. sugar
2 oz. chocolate powder
3 oz. ground almonds
little whipped cream
cherries

1 Line patty tins with the pastry.
2 Prick and bake 'blind' in a hot oven (450 °F. – Gas Mark 7) about 8 minutes until set, but not browned.
3 Whisk egg whites, add other ingredients, put into pastry cases and bake for further 10–12 minutes in moderate oven.
4 When cold pipe border of cream, decorate with pieces of cherry.

Chocolate cake

Cooking time made in minutes

You will need:

4 oz. margarine
1 tablespoon cocoa
few cherries and walnuts to decorate
4 oz. sugar
1 egg
8 oz. broken sweet biscuits

1 Crush the biscuits with a rolling pin.
2 Melt the margarine and sugar together in a saucepan.
3 Add the cocoa.
4 Remove from the heat and add the egg, mixing quickly.
5 Stir in the broken biscuits.
6 Turn into a greased loaf tin and press down.
7 Leave to set. Turn out and decorate with cherries and walnuts.

Chocolate cake

No cooking

You will need:

3 oz. butter
1 oz. castor sugar
glacé icing
1 tablespoon golden syrup
4 oz. plain chocolate
8 oz. digestive biscuits

1 Crush biscuits into fine crumbs.
2 Brush a 7-inch flan ring with a little melted butter and place it on a flat dish.
3 Cream the butter, sugar and syrup, add melted chocolate and biscuit crumbs.
4 Pack mixture into ring, smoothing the top.
5 Chill for at least 3 hours.
6 Remove flan ring.
7 Coat cake with lemon or orange-flavoured glacé icing and decorate with grated chocolate.

Chocolate surprise cookies

Cooking time 12 minutes

You will need:

8 oz. flour (with plain flour use 2 level teaspoons baking powder)
2 oz. chocolate
4 oz. margarine
5 oz. sugar
1 egg
little milk

1 Sieve flour, rub in margarine, add sugar, egg and enough milk to mix.
2 Put in small heaps in lightly greased and floured tins.
3 Make a hole in the centre of each cookie.
4 Put a piece of chocolate in each hole and almost cover with the cake mixture.
5 Bake for 10–12 minutes in hot oven (425–450 °F.—Gas Mark 6–7).

Coffee japs

Cooking time   40 minutes

You will need:

3 egg whites	6 oz. ground almonds
6 oz. castor sugar	

for the filling

1 tablespoon coffee essence	4 oz. butter or margarine
	6 oz. sieved icing sugar

for the icing

1 tablespoon coffee essence	approximately 6 oz. sieved icing sugar
	hazel nuts to decorate

1 Whisk the egg whites until stiff, add the sugar and the ground almonds.
2 Line a small Swiss roll tin with oiled paper, spread with the mixture and bake in the centre of a very moderate oven (350°F.—Gas Mark 3) until the cake begins to turn golden, approximately 20 minutes.
3 Take out of the oven, mark about 18 or 20 small rounds, as close together as possible so none of the cake is wasted.
4 Return to the oven and cook for about another 15 minutes.
5 Lift the rounds out carefully, and return the 'trimmings' to the oven for a further few minutes to brown more.
6 Make the filling by creaming butter and icing sugar and adding the essence very gradually, so the mixture does not curdle.
7 Sandwich the little cakes together with the coffee butter icing and spread some round the outside.
8 Crush the 'trimmings' to make crumbs and coat the sides of the cakes liberally.
9 Cover the tops with coffee icing and decorate with a hazel nut.

Continental cheese cake

No cooking

Another delicious continental cheese cake is made by splitting a sponge cake into 3 layers and spreading each layer with the following: 8 oz. cottage or cream cheese creamed with 2 oz. castor sugar, 2 oz. grated chocolate and a little maraschino or sherry.

Cornflake cookies

Cooking time   20 minutes

You will need:

2 egg whites	1 oz. ground almonds
3 oz. desiccated coconut	2 oz. crumbled cornflakes
	few cherries
5 oz. sugar	rice paper

1 Whisk egg whites, add coconut, almonds, cornflakes, sugar and pile on to rice paper with a cherry on each.

2 Bake for 18–20 minutes in centre of very moderate oven (350°F.—Gas Mark 3).

Cornflake and coconut macaroons

Cooking time   15 minutes

You will need:

2 large egg whites	1 oz. crushed cornflakes
pinch of salt	2 oz. ground almonds
2 oz. desiccated coconut	3 oz. castor sugar
	few drops almond essence

1 Whisk egg whites, add all other ingredients.
2 Knead well and put into small paper cases. This makes about 16–18 cakes.
3 Bake for 15 minutes in centre of moderate oven (375°F.—Gas Mark 5) until golden brown.

Cream layer cookies

Cooking time   10 minutes

You will need:

8 oz. flour	little cochineal
5 oz. margarine	whipped cream
5 oz. castor sugar	angelica
egg	

1 Cream margarine and sugar until soft and light.
2 Add flour, knead well and work in enough egg to bind.
3 Colour $\frac{1}{3}$ of the dough pink, with cochineal.
4 Roll out until under $\frac{1}{4}$ inch thick, cut into rounds and bake on ungreased tins for about 10 minutes in moderate oven (375°F.—Gas Mark 4).
5 Cool on baking tins.
6 Sandwich 3 of these biscuits with whipped cream and decorate with whipped cream and angelica, putting a pink biscuit between 2 white ones.

Feather cream cakes

Cooking time   15 minutes

You will need:

3 oz. butter	5 oz. flour (with plain flour use $1\frac{1}{4}$ teaspoons baking powder)
3 oz. castor sugar	
icing sugar to decorate	
2 eggs	1 tablespoon cream (top of milk)

1 Cream butter and sugar very well indeed.
2 Gradually add well-beaten eggs, then fold in sieved flour and cream.
3 Put into greased and floured patty tins and bake for about 12–15 minutes in moderately hot oven (400°F.—Gas Mark 5).
4 Dust with icing sugar if wished.

Variations on previous recipe overleaf:

variations on Feather cream cakes

Queen Cakes: Add 1 oz. currants.

Coconut Cakes: Use 1 oz. coconut instead of 1 oz. flour.

Chocolate Cakes: Omit 1 oz. flour and use 1 oz. chocolate powder.

French cinnamon tea-cake

Cooking time	20–25 minutes

You will need:

1 egg	few drops vanilla essence
2 oz. castor sugar	4 oz. flour (with plain
1 tablespoon melted	flour 1 teaspoon baking
butter	powder)
4 tablespoons milk	

topping

melted butter	1 level teaspoon cinnamon
	(or alternatively spice)

1 Separate egg yolk from white.
2 Whisk egg white till stiff and peaky then gradually whisk in sugar, followed by yolk.
3 Fold in milk and essence and lastly flour and butter.
4 Turn mixture into well-greased 7-inch sandwich tin.
5 Bake towards top of oven (375°F.—Gas Mark 4) for 20–25 minutes.
6 Remove from oven, brush top with melted butter and sprinkle with cinnamon.
7 Serve warm with butter, clotted cream or cottage cheese and jam or honey.
8 Instead of the butter and spice top, this tea cake can be topped while warm with soft lemon icing and finely chopped walnuts.

Jiffy gingerbread

Cooking time	1 hour

You will need:

3 oz. cooking fat or	2 oz. sugar (brown or
margarine	white)
8 oz. golden syrup or	¼ gill of water or milk
treacle (or mix these	8 oz. flour (with plain
two)	flour 1 teaspoon baking
1 LEVEL teaspoon	powder)
bicarbonate of soda	1–1½ teaspoons
4 oz. sultanas or raisins	powdered ginger
	1 egg

1 Heat fat, sugar, syrup and water in a large pan until fat has melted.
2 ALLOW TO COOL.
3 Sieve flour and all dry ingredients together.
4 Add to ingredients in saucepan and beat well.
5 Stir in egg and sultanas.
6 Pour into 7-inch tin lined with greased greaseproof paper and bake in the centre of a very moderate oven (350°F.—Gas Mark 3) for approximately 1 hour.
7 Cool in tin a short time before turning out.

Lemon jumbles

Cooking time	10 minutes

You will need:

4 oz. margarine	8 oz. flour (with plain
4 oz. sugar	flour use 2 level
1 egg	teaspoons baking
	powder)
	grated rind of 2 lemons
	lemon juice to mix

1 Sieve flour and baking powder together.
2 Rub in the margarine, add the sugar and lemon rind.
3 Mix in the egg and enough lemon juice to make a firm dough.
4 Roll out the dough until it is ¼ inch thick.
5 Cut into long strips and make these into bows.
6 Put on to a lightly greased and floured baking tin.
7 Bake for 10 minutes near the top of a very hot oven (475°F.—Gas Mark 8).
8 Brush top with a thin layer of lemon-flavoured water icing, made by mixing 4 tablespoons icing sugar with 1 tablespoon lemon juice.
9 Put cherries and angelica into centre.

Macaroon animals

Cooking time	20 minutes

You will need:

2 egg whites	about 2 teaspoons
6 oz. ground almonds	cornflour
6 oz. castor sugar	little icing for decoration

1 Whisk egg whites lightly, add ground almonds, sugar and enough cornflour to make firm dough.
2 Roll out to thin dough, cut into shapes with animal cutters.
3 Put on rice paper or baking tins and bake for about 20 minutes in a very moderate oven (350°F.—Gas Mark 3).
4 Cut round paper when cold.
5 Decorate with icing.

Macaroon fingers

Cooking time	20 minutes

You will need:

whites of 2 eggs	6 oz. sugar
6 oz. ground almonds	few drops orange
finely grated rind of	flavoured water
2 oranges	rice paper

1 Mix all ingredients together.
2 Form into finger shapes on rice paper on baking trays.
3 Bake for approximately 18–20 minutes in centre of moderate oven (375°F.—Gas Mark 4).
4 Cut around biscuits.
5 When cold they can either be covered with orange flavoured water icing and chopped nuts or left plain.

Mincemeat cookies

Cooking time   15 minutes

You will need:

4 oz. margarine	little egg yolk
4 oz. sugar	2 or 3 tablespoons
icing sugar	mincemeat
8 oz. plain flour	

1 Cream the margarine and sugar.
2 Work in flour and just enough egg yolk to bind it.
3 Cut into rounds and cut a circle from the centre of half the rounds.
4 Put the complete rounds on to baking trays. place the rings firmly on top.
5 Fill the centre with mincemeat.
6 Bake for about 15 minutes at 375°F.—Gas Mark 4.
7 Cool on the tin.
8 Dredge the outer ring with icing sugar.

Mocha flapjacks

Cooking time   25–30 minutes

You will need for 12 flapjacks:

2 oz. butter or	4 oz. rolled oats
margarine	2 oz. golden syrup
2 oz. roughly chopped	2 oz. chopped walnuts
chocolate	2 teaspoons coffee
	essence

1 Melt butter. syrup and coffee essence together in saucepan.
2 Add rolled oats.
3 Mix well and allow to cool slightly.
4 Fold in chopped nuts and chocolate.
5 Spread mixture evenly in lightly greased 7-inch square cake tin.
6 Cook on middle shelf, very moderate oven (350°F.—Gas Mark 3) for 25–30 minutes.
7 Cut in portions, while warm, allow to cool slightly. Remove carefully.

Orange tarts

Cooking time   15–20 minutes

You will need:

4–5 oz. short crust	little marmalade
pastry (see page 86)	
for filling	
1 oz. butter	3 oz. marmalade
1 egg	3 oz. soft cake crumbs

1 Line patty tins with pastry and add a little marmalade.
2 Cream butter and marmalade, gradually beat in egg and crumbs.
3 Put mixture into tart cases and bake for 15–20 minutes in the centre of a moderately hot oven (400°F.–Gas Mark 5).
4 If desired, top with a little icing, made by combining icing sugar with enough orange juice to give spreading consistency.

Peanut butter cookies

Cooking time   10–12 minutes

You will need:

2 oz. self-raising flour	1 oz. fine semolina
pinch of salt	2 oz. butter or margarine
2 oz. peanut butter	2 oz. soft brown sugar
few drops vanilla	1 egg
essence	

1 Sift together flour. semolina and salt.
2 Cream fat, sugar, peanut butter and vanilla essence together until light.
3 Beat in egg, then stir in the dry ingredients.
4 Drop teaspoons of mixture. 1 inch apart. on to ungreased baking trays.
5 Bake in a moderate oven (375°F.—Gas Mark 4) for 10–12 minutes.
6 Cool on a wire tray. Store in an airtight container.
7 Makes approximately 24 cookies.

Pineapple cherry cookies

Cooking time   15 minutes

You will need:

3 oz. margarine	4 oz. flour (with plain flour
2 oz. sugar	1 teaspoon baking
1 oz. chopped glacé	powder)
cherries	cherries and pineapple to
1 oz. chopped glacé	decorate
pineapple	

1 Cream margarine and sugar.
2 Stir in pineapple. cherries and sieved flour.
3 Roll into balls.
4 Put on to lightly greased and floured baking trays with room to spread.
5 Put a piece of cherry and pineapple on top.
6 Bake for 15 minutes in centre of moderate oven (375°F.—Gas Mark 4).
7 Cool on tin.

Pineapple Madeleines

Cooking time   15 minutes

You will need:

pineapple jam	3 oz. castor sugar
coconut	4 oz. flour (with plain flour
glacé pineapple	use 1 level teaspoon
2 eggs	baking powder)
3 oz. margarine	1 packet pineapple-
	flavoured cornflour

1 Cream margarine and sugar.
2 Add eggs and sieved flour and cornflour.
3 Half fill greased and floured dariole tins.
4 Bake for 15 minutes in centre of oven (400°F.—Gas Mark 5).
5 When cold, coat with pineapple jam and coconut and decorate with piece of glacé pineapple.

Raisin doughnuts

Cooking time   6 minutes

You will need:

4 oz. flour (with plain flour use 1½ level teaspoons baking powder)	2–3 oz. lard for frying
	2 oz. raisins
	1 oz. sugar
½ gill milk	1 egg
	little castor sugar for coating

1 Sieve flour, add other ingredients and beat until a smooth, thick batter.
2 Heat lard in frying pan and drop in spoonfuls of mixture.
3 Cook steadily for about 3 minutes until golden, turn and cook other side.
4 Drain on crumpled tissue paper for 1 minute then roll in castor sugar.

Rock buns

Cooking time   10 minutes

You will need:

8 oz. flour (with plain flour use 2½ teaspoons baking powder)	6 oz. dried fruit
	5 oz. margarine
	5 oz. sugar
	1 egg
	2 oz. candied peel

1 Sieve flour and baking powder together.
2 Rub in margarine, add sugar, beaten egg and enough milk to make a stiff consistency. Be careful not to make the mixture too soft or the buns will spread badly.
3 Add the fruit and peel.
4 Grease and flour baking tins and put small heaps of the mixture on these, dusting lightly with sugar.
5 Bake for 10 minutes near the top of a hot to very hot oven (450–475°F.—Gas Mark 7–8). If the oven is inclined to be rather fierce, lower the heat after the first 5 minutes.

Variation
Omit dried fruit. Put in heaps on the baking trays. Make a small hole in the centre of each and put in a spoonful of jam—apricot or raspberry being the most suitable.

Sponge cakes

Cooking time   20–25 minutes

You will need:

6 oz. margarine	2–3 eggs
6 oz. castor sugar	8 oz. self-raising flour
little milk	few drops vanilla essence

1 Cream the margarine and sugar with the vanilla essence until soft and light.
2 Gradually beat in the eggs, stir in the flour, well sieved, and enough milk to make a soft consistency.
3 Put the mixture into a Swiss roll tin (lined with greaseproof paper, greased with margarine and lightly floured).
4 Bake for approximately 20–25 minutes in a moderate oven (375–400°F.—Gas Mark 4–5).
5 Serve plain, cut in fingers, or try the following variations:

Chocolate walnuts

You will need:

2 oz. margarine	2 teaspoons chocolate powder
3 oz. sieved icing sugar	walnut halves
chopped walnuts	

1 Make icing by creaming margarine and sieved icing sugar with chocolate powder.
2 Coat sides and tops of sponge fingers.
3 Roll in chopped walnuts.
4 Decorate with piped border of chocolate icing and walnut halves.

Pineapple diamonds

You will need:

pineapple jam	crystallized pineapple
whipped cream	

1 Cut cake into diamond-shapes, and cut these in half.
2 Spread with pineapple jam, sandwich together.
3 Coat and decorate the tops of the cake with whipped cream.
4 Decorate with crystallized pineapple.

Winter shortcake

Cooking time   20 minutes

You will need:

4 oz. margarine	1 egg
4 oz. castor sugar	6 oz. self-raising flour
whipped cream	fruit salad

1 Cream together the margarine and sugar.
2 Add the egg and sieved flour.
3 Divide the mixture between two 7-inch lightly-greased and floured sandwich tins.
4 Flatten the mixture with very slightly damped fingers.
5 Bake for about 20 minutes at 400°F.—Gas Mark 5.
6 Turn out and when cold, sandwich together and decorate with whipped cream and chopped canned fruit salad.

Bridge rolls

Cooking time   15 minutes

You will need:

8 oz. plain flour	4 level teaspoons baking powder
½ oz. lard	
½ level teaspoon salt	¼ pint milk (for use as required)
1 egg	

1 Sieve together plain flour, baking powder and salt.
2 Lightly rub in the lard.
3 Make a well in the centre, add the egg and some of the milk.
4 Fold in the flour gently to make an elastic dough, adding more milk if necessary.
5 Turn on to a floured board and divide into 8.
6 Shape into rolls.
7 Bake 15 minutes on lightly greased baking tin near top of hot oven (450–475 °F.—Gas Mark 7–8).
8 Cool on a wire tray.

Rich cheese scones

Cooking time   10 minutes

You will need:

8 oz. flour (with plain flour use 4 level teaspoons baking powder)	good pinch salt, pepper, mustard
	2 oz. butter
	4 oz. grated cheese
little milk to mix	1 egg

1 Sieve dry ingredients.
2 Rub in butter.
3 Add cheese, leaving a little to glaze scones.
4 Bind with egg and milk to soft rolling consistency.
5 Roll out dough to ½ inch thick and cut into shapes.
6 Brush with milk or egg and top with grated cheese.
7 Bake for good 10 minutes in hot oven (425–450°F.—Gas Mark 6–7).

Herb scones

Cooking time   12 minutes

You will need:

8 oz. self-raising flour	1 level teaspoon mixed herbs
2 oz. margarine	
½ level teaspoon salt	
approximately 6 tablespoons milk	

1 Sift flour and salt into a bowl.
2 Rub in margarine.
3 Add herbs, then mix to a soft, but not sticky dough with the milk.
4 Turn out on a lightly floured board.
5 Knead quickly till smooth, then roll out to about ½ inch in thickness.
6 Cut into 4 rounds with a 3½–4 inch plain cutter or, pressing dough to round shape, cut across into 4 to 6 triangles.
7 Transfer to a greased baking sheet.
8 Brush tops with milk, then bake towards top of hot oven (450°F.—Gas Mark 7) for 12 minutes.

9 Split open while hot and serve with butter and Cheddar cheese, or with a casserole of steak or ham.

Quickie rolls

Cooking time   12 minutes

You will need:

8 oz. self-raising flour (with plain flour use 2 level teaspoons baking powder)	salt
	1 oz. margarine
	milk to mix

1 Sieve flour and salt, rub in the margarine and mix with enough milk to make a firm dough.
2 Roll out to smooth dough, a good ¼ inch thick.
3 Cut into long strips, then roll up each strip like a tiny Swiss roll.
4 Put these strips into greased patty tins, brush the tops with milk and bake for about 12 minutes in a hot oven (450°F,—Gas Mark 7).

Raisin and walnut scones

Cooking time   10 minutes

You will need:

6 oz. self-raising flour	1½ oz. margarine
salt	2 tablespoons raisins
1 tablespoon brown sugar	1 tablespoon chopped walnuts
milk to mix	

1 Sieve flour and salt together.
2 Rub in the margarine, add all other ingredients, making a dough of a soft roll consistency.
3 Roll out to ½ inch thick.
4 Cut into small rounds, put on to a lightly greased baking tray and bake for 10 minutes (475°F.—Gas Mark 8).

Spiced Scotch pancakes

Cooking time   4 minutes

You will need:

1 oz. margarine	1 egg
4 oz. self-raising flour	¼ pint milk
½ teaspoon mixed spice	

1 Sieve flour with spice, add the egg and gradually stir in the milk to make a smooth, thick batter.
2 Lastly, add the melted margarine.
3 Heat a griddle or frying pan and rub lightly with margarine.
4 Drop spoonfuls of the mixture on this and cook for about 2 minutes until the top side 'bubbles'.
5 Turn carefully and cook them for about the same time on the second side.

Short crust pastry

You will need:

8 oz. flour
4 oz. fat*
good pinch salt

cold water to mix—
approximately
2 tablespoons

*There are many fats and combinations of fats that give a first class short crust pastry. Choose between:

Modern whipped light fat. Use 3½ oz. only as it is very rich.

Pure cooking fat or lard.

Margarine—for best results use a table margarine, a superfine or luxury margarine.

Butter or perhaps the favourite of all—2 oz. margarine and 2 oz. cooking fat.

1 Sieve flour and salt and rub in fat until mixture looks like fine breadcrumbs.
2 Using first a knife and then the fingertips to feel the pastry, gradually add enough cold water to make the dough of a rolling consistency.
3 Lightly flour the rolling-pin and pastry board. If a great deal of flour is necessary to roll out the pastry then you have undoubtedly made it too wet.
4 Roll pastry to required thickness and shape, lifting and turning to keep it light.
5 Exact cooking times for pastry are given in the recipes but as a general rule it should be cooked in a hot oven (425–450°F.—or Gas Mark 6–7).

Rich short crust

As short crust pastry, but use butter and bind with egg yolk and a little water.

Sweet short crust

You will need:

8 oz. flour
5 oz. butter*
2 oz. sugar

pinch salt
egg yolk to bind

*Table, luxury or superfine margarine can be used.

1 Cream fat and sugar together until light in colour.
2 Sieve flour and salt together and add to creamed fat, mixing with a knife.
3 Gradually add enough water or egg and water to make a firm rolling consistency. Use fingertips to feel the pastry.
4 To line flan put pastry over case and press down base and sides firmly then roll over top with rolling-pin for a good edge.
5 Decorate edge as wished.

Chapter 9   Entertaining

It is a great pity if lack of time stops one entertaining at home for 'easy to prepare' parties can be just as enjoyable as more ambitious ones. In this chapter are ideas for quick and easy sweet or savoury dishes which look attractive yet take a short time only to prepare.

Appetizers *for cocktail parties*

Made in a minute appetizers that need no cooking.

Raw cauliflower sprigs—well washed, are delicious if rolled in celery salt and grated Parmesan cheese.

Heat processed cheese in a colourful basin over hot water and serve with potato crisps.

Sardine fingers. Cut fingers of bread and spread with tomato butter, i.e. cream equal quantities of margarine and tomato ketchup. Top with sardines and garnish with grated Parmesan cheese and chopped parsley.

Liver sausage canapés. Mash liver sausage with tomato ketchup or chutney. Spread on small cocktail biscuits and pipe border of stars with cream cheese. Garnish with rings of gherkin.

Prawn canapés. Mix margarine with a little mayonnaise and a small quantity of finely chopped parsley or watercress. Spread on tiny rounds of bread or biscuits and press prawns on top.

Surprise cheese balls. Roll a little soft cream cheese round tiny cocktail onions, then toss in chopped parsley and red pepper. Put cocktail stick through each ball.

Asparagus fingers. Dip short canned or cooked frozen asparagus heads into a little mayonnaise. Put on thin slices of brown bread—spread with butter and roll firmly.

Cheese life-savers

Cooking time   15 minutes

You will need:

sliced white bread (day-old)	finely grated cheese
	pinch cayenne pepper
butter	1 large carrot

1 Cut circles from the sliced bread using a 1¾-inch pastry-cutter and remove the centres using a 1-inch cutter.
2 Melt a little butter in a frying pan, dip the bread rings in the butter then toss in the finely grated seasoned cheese until well coated.
3 Use Cheddar to which a little Parmesan may be added for extra flavour.
4 Place the cheese-coated bread on a baking sheet and brown in a moderately hot oven (400°F.—Gas Mark 5) taking about 10 minutes.
5 Serve at once.
6 Trim the base of a large clean carrot and stand it upright with cocktail sticks prodded diagonally into the top part – hand the Life-savers on the sticks.

Cheese meringues

Cooking time   10 minutes

You will need:

2 egg whites	good pinch each of
2 tablespoons finely grated cheese	salt
(preferably Parmesan)	pepper
little cooking fat for frying	dry mustard

1 Whisk egg whites stiffly.
2 Fold in seasoning and cheese.
3 Make sure fat is really hot, then drop in small spoonfuls of cheese mixture.
4 Cook each meringue for 2 or 3 minutes until crisp and golden.
5 Drain on crumpled tissue paper and serve at once.
6 Delicious with a drink or as a light snack in the evening.

Cheese savouries

(Six hot savouries)

Cooking time   5–15 minutes

For these, you can use Cheddar cheese, or, even better, petit Gruyère triangles.

1 Dip triangles of cheese in fritter batter and fry.
2 Egg and crumb cheese triangles, then fry. Split, and put together again with a slice of ham or ham paste.
3 Sandwich cheese between slices of bread, soak in beaten egg for a few minutes, then fry.
4 Sandwich thin slivers of cheese between thinly rolled short pastry, seal the edges, brush pastry with beaten egg and bake for 15 minutes in hot oven.
5 Put slices of cheese on buttered bread spread with anchovy paste, and toast under grill.
6 Put slice of cheese on buttered bread, sprinkle with paprika and put in a hot oven until golden brown.

Cheese and salad platter

No cooking

You will need:

selection of cheese, Cheddar, Gruyère, Caerphilly	tiny RAW cut cauliflower
	cold new potatoes (left from another meal)
tomatoes	cooked carrots (or use canned carrots)
2 hard-boiled eggs	
mayonnaise	mint
parsley	lettuce
vinegar	oil
seasoning	

1 Chop hard-boiled egg yolk.
2 Arrange cheese on bed of lettuce.
3 Divide cauliflower into neat sprigs, coat with mayonnaise and egg yolk.
4 Mix new potatoes with mint and mayonnaise.
5 Toss carrots in oil, vinegar, seasonings and chopped parsley.
6 Garnish with rings of egg whites.
7 Slice tomatoes, top with chopped parsley.

Cheese squares

No cooking time
You will need:

bread
butter
cream cheese
cornflakes

1 Cut fresh bread into 1-inch cubes.
2 Spread all sides first with butter, then with cream cheese.
3 Toss in cornflakes until completely covered.

Date and cream cheese delights

(makes 10–18, depending on size)
No cooking
You will need:

4 oz. cream cheese
1 oz. brown sugar
1 dessertspoon golden syrup
1–2 oz. crushed or
chopped nuts for decoration
6 oz. dates (cut fine)
2 teaspoons grated orange rind
2 oz. rolled oats

1 Crush nuts.
2 Put cheese, sugar, syrup, orange rind, dates and rolled oats in mixing bowl.
3 Cream thoroughly together.
4 Chill (in a refrigerator if you like).
5 Shape into balls.
6 Roll in crushed nuts.
7 Place in paper cases.

Stuffed dates

Take stones out of firm dates and fill centres with soft cream cheese.

Stuffed prunes

Stone cooked and well-drained prunes and fill centres with cheese mixed with chopped nuts.

Meat popovers

Cooking time   15 minutes
You will need:

4 oz. flaked or chopped ham or corned beef or cooked bacon
a batter made with 2 oz. flour
1 egg
$\frac{1}{3}$ gill milk
seasoning

1 Add the flaked or chopped ham, corned beef or cooked bacon to the batter.
2 Put a little fat in deep patty tins and get this very hot, pour in the mixture and bake for about 10–15 minutes near the top of a hot oven (450°F.—Gas Mark 7).
3 Serve hot with crisp salad.

Wine and cheese party

One of the easiest and most popular parties of today is a cheese and wine buffet.
Choose a good selection of cheeses on 1 or 2 plates or boards:
Fairly mild cheese: Cheddar, Cheshire.
A soft cheese like Camembert or Brie.
Cream cheese like Demi-sel or Cottage cheese.
Biting cheese: Danish blue, Stilton, Gorganzola. Have plenty of French bread, crisp bread, biscuits, butter.
Dishes of celery and apples or crisp lettuce.
Serve a good red Burgundy—such as a Beaujolais or Mâcon at room temperature and a white Burgundy—Chablis ⎱slightly or white Bordeaux—dry Graves ⎰chilled

Autumn glory sundae

No cooking time
You will need:

1 family brick ice-cream
a few blackberries
angelica or small mint
leaves to garnish
4–6 tablespoons blackberry brandy (or blackberry syrup)

1 Place spoonsfuls of ice-cream into 4–6 glasses.
2 Pour blackberry brandy over each portion then add more ice-cream.
3 Scatter blackberries over the top of each ice and add mint leaves or leaves of angelica by each berry.
4 Serve at once.

Baked oranges with ice-cream

Cooking time   15 minutes

1 block of ice-cream
2 oz. sugar
little lemon juice or
sherry
4 oranges
1 oz. butter

1 Peel and slice the oranges into rings.
2 Put into a shallow dish with the butter, sugar and lemon juice or sherry and bake for about 15 minutes in a moderately hot oven (400°F. —Gas Mark 5).
3 Arrange round the block of ice-cream.
4 The oranges should be very hot to form a good contrast to the ice-cream.

Banana fluff

No Cooking
You will need:

5 bananas
$\frac{1}{4}$ pint cream
2 egg whites
2 tablespoons icing sugar
about 12 sponge fingers
little lemon juice

1 Whisk cream until stiff and egg whites until very stiff.
2 Mash 4 bananas with sugar and lemon juice. Fold cream into this, then add egg whites.
3 Line shallow dish with the sponge fingers and pile banana mixture on top.
4 Decorate with remaining banana.
5 Try this with fresh raspberries or strawberries when a luxury sweet is required.

Chocolate almond mousse

Cooking time	8–10 minutes

4 oz. plain chocolate	2 oz. chopped blanched
little cream or top of	almonds
milk	sponge cake
2 eggs	

1 Chop the chocolate into small pieces.
2 Dissolve in a basin over hot water.
3 Add the yolks of the eggs and 2 tablespoons cream or milk.
4 Whisk or beat over hot water, until thick and creamy.
5 Cool, then add chopped almonds and whisked egg whites.
6 Put into glasses and serve with fingers of sponge.

And mocha mousse

Recipe as above but use strong coffee instead of cream and, if wished, add a little sugar.

Chocolate ice-cream pie

Cooking time	8–10 minutes

You will need for 6–8 servings:

approximately 8 oz.	4 oz. butter
chocolate wholemeal	1 vanilla ice-cream block
biscuits	1 strawberry ice-cream
small piece of plain or	block (both large size
milk chocolate	blocks)
little whipped cream	

1 Put the biscuits on a piece of greaseproof paper, cover with another piece of paper and roll firmly until fine crumbs.
2 Mix in a basin with the cool melted butter and form into a flan shape in a dish.
3 If wished you can put into a very moderate oven (350°F.—Gas Mark 3) for about 8–10 minutes to give added crispness, but the biscuit flan is perfectly all right if not cooked at all.
4 Allow to cool and when ready to serve, fill with vanilla and strawberry ice-creams, spreading these slightly so you have a 'streaky' effect.
5 Top with whipped cream and coarsely grated chocolate.

6 You can prepare the filling before your meal if you put the pie into the coldest part of the refrigerator.

Coupe Jacques mixed fruit sundae

No cooking

ice-cream	blanched almonds
fruit salad—fresh or	canned or maraschino
canned	cherries
whipped cream	
Melba sauce (see page	
72)	

1 Chop and brown the almonds lightly under the grill or in the oven.
2 Arrange the fruit and ice-cream in individual glasses.
3 Top with a little Melba sauce, nuts, cream and cherries.

Delicious chestnut mousse

for a special occasion

Cooking time	10 minutes

You will need:

1 lb. chestnuts (or use	2 eggs
chestnut purée)	$\frac{1}{4}$ pint cream
$\frac{1}{2}$ gill water	1 teaspoon powder
2 oz. sugar	gelatine

to decorate

little grated	vanilla essence
chocolate	crystallized violet petals

1 Slit the skins so they do not burst, rub through sieve after boiling steadily for 10 minutes.
2 Separate eggs.
3 Beat egg yolks and sugar over hot water until thick, dissolve gelatine in the $\frac{1}{2}$ gill very hot water, add to egg yolks.
4 Stir in chestnut purée and vanilla essence.
5 When stiffening, fold in cream and stiffly beaten egg whites.
6 Pile into glasses and top with crystallized violet petals and a little grated chocolate.

Fried peaches

Cooking time	3 minutes

You will need:

4 large fresh or 8 halves	2 oz. butter
of canned peaches	2 oz. sugar
little rum or brandy	
for special occasions	

1 Heat the butter and add the peaches sprinkled with rum or brandy.
2 Cook steadily for about 3 minutes, adding the sugar.
3 Serve when the sugar has melted and given a brown sauce.
4 Ice-cream or cream makes this a wonderful sweet.

Fruits flambés

Cooking time   5–10 minutes

1 Heat plenty of butter in a frying pan, then dust halves of skinned pears, peaches, etc., with brown sugar.
2 Toss in the hot butter until golden on the outside.
3 Lift on to a hot plate—pour over warmed brandy or Curaçao and ignite.
4 Serve at once.

Orange chocolate pie

Cooking time   few minutes

You will need for 4–6 servings:

6 oz. digestive biscuits	1 oz. butter
3 oz. plain chocolate, grated	$\frac{1}{2}$ orange jelly
2 teaspoons lemon juice	1 small can evaporated milk
	cream (optional)

1 Put the biscuits between 2 sheets of greaseproof paper or foil, crush them into fine crumbs with rolling pin.
2 Heat the butter and 2 oz. chocolate in a basin over a pan of hot water until melted.
3 Put the biscuit crumbs in a bowl, pour in the chocolate and butter and mix well with a fork.
4 Line the base and sides of a buttered 8-inch pie-plate or sandwich tin with the mixture. Press firmly into position.
5 Meanwhile, dissolve the jelly in a little hot water.
6 Make up to $\frac{1}{4}$ pint, leave in a cold place.
7 Whisk the milk with the lemon juice until thick.
8 When the jelly is almost setting, add it to the milk, whisking throughout.
9 Pile the mixture into the prepared case.
10 Leave to set. Decorate with remaining chocolate, and cream if used.

Peach surprise

No cooking

You will need:

2 large fresh peaches or 4 peach halves from canned fruit	4 thin slices of Swiss roll or pieces of sponge cake
small pieces of preserved or crystallized ginger	little whipped cream few maraschino cherries or canned cherries and syrup
1 tablespoon ground almonds	whipped cream

1 Skin peaches by dipping them first into very hot water for a few seconds only, then into cold water.

2 Halve and remove stones.
3 Put the Swiss roll on to dishes and soak lightly with cherry syrup.
4 Mix about 2–3 tablespoons whipped cream with cherries, finely chopped ginger and ground almonds. Sweeten if wished.
5 Press into centre of peaches in place of the stones and turn upside-down on Swiss roll.
6 Pipe cream round fruit, decorate with cherries and serve with ice-cream.

Peach Melba

No cooking

Peach and other fruit Melbas are made in the same way as Strawberry Melba (see page 91). Use skinned fresh, or canned peaches. If using fresh peaches lower gently into boiling water for 30 seconds. Lift into cold water and skin.
Do not skin too soon before serving or the fruit will turn a bad colour.

Raspberry sponge mould

No cooking

You will need:

1 packet frozen or 1 can raspberries	6 sponge cakes (small sugar ones)
3 good-sized eating apples	sugar to taste

1 Drain away surplus juice from canned raspberries; keep this to add to jellies or fruit drinks.
2 Line the sides and bottom of a mould with sliced sponge cake. Keep some for the top.
3 Peel and grate the apples, mix the raspberries and a very little sugar if wished.
4 Pack into the sponge-lined mould and cover with more sponge cake.
5 Put a saucer or small plate on top and a weight and leave overnight.
6 Top with remaining fruit.
7 This is excellent served with ice-cream.

Rum and coffee gâteau

No cooking

You will need:

1 sponge round about 7 inches in diameter (it can be a stale cake)	2–4 oz. split walnuts
	4–5 oz. butter
1 tablespoon rum	4–5 oz. sugar (castor)
$\frac{1}{2}$ pint strong coffee	2 egg yolks
	little water icing

1 Line a cake tin, the same size as the sponge cake, with greased paper.
2 Split the cake across to make about 4 layers.
3 Cream together the butter and sugar until very soft and light.
4 Work in the 2 egg yolks, 1 gill of the coffee and the rum.
5 The mixture will doubtless have a curdled appearance, but this does not matter.
6 Put 1 layer sponge cake in the bottom of the tin.
7 Pour over enough coffee to moisten this.
8 Spread with a thin layer of the coffee mixture.
9 Put the next layer of sponge over the top, moisten with coffee and spread with coffee mixture.
10 Continue in this way until you put on the top layer of sponge.
11 Simply moisten this with coffee.
12 Put a piece of paper over the top of the cake and put a weight on top. Leave overnight.
13 Remove the weight and paper and gently pour away any coffee that may have come to the top of the cake.
14 Turn out of tin.
15 Cover the top with a water icing and decorate with halved walnuts.

1 Arrange the fruit and ice-cream in individual glasses.
2 Top with Melba sauce, rosettes of whipped cream and chopped blanched almonds.

Pears suprême

Cooking time   8 minutes

You will need:

8 canned pear halves	2 oz. blanched almonds
¼ pint pear syrup from can	¼ pint red wine
2 tablespoons redcurrant jelly	cream

1 Put the jelly, wine and syrup into a saucepan and heat until the jelly has melted.
2 Arrange the pears in a shallow dish, together with the almonds, pour over the wine sauce and allow to cool.
3 Serve with cream or ice-cream.

Strawberry Alaska

Cooking time   3–5 minutes

You will need:

1 sponge cake	1 packet frozen
5 egg whites	strawberries
block of ice-cream	5 oz. castor sugar

1 Put the sponge cake into a dish and soak it well with strawberry syrup.
2 Arrange the strawberries on top with the firm ice-cream.
3 Put egg whites into a basin and whisk until very firm.
4 Fold in the sugar.
5 Pile the meringue over the top of ice-cream and fruit and bake for 3–5 minutes in a very hot oven (475–500°F.—Gas Mark 8–9).

Frosted peaches

No cooking

You will need:

8 canned peach halves	1 oz. chopped Maraschino
1 oz. chopped nuts	cherries
1 oz. ground almonds	8 Maraschino cherries to
¼ pint thick cream	decorate

1 Whip the cream lightly, then add the ground almonds, cherries and nuts.
2 Put the halved peaches, together with the syrup from the can into the freezing trays of a refrigerator.
3 Fill with the cream mixture, and top with the cherries.
4 Frost for approximately 25 minutes, then serve with the lightly frozen syrup round the halved peaches.
5 DO NOT FREEZE for any longer, otherwise the fruit will be too hard.

Strawberry Melba

No cooking

You will need:

ice-cream	strawberries
Melba sauce (see page 72)	blanched almonds
	whipped cream

Frosted pears

Recipe as above, but use chopped ginger instead of nuts.

Index